The Reason Why the Colored American Is Not in the World's Columbian Exposition

THE
REASON WHY

the Colored American
Is Not in the World's Columbian
Exposition

The Afro-American's Contribution
to Columbian Literature

Ida B. Wells,
Frederick Douglass,
Irvine Garland Penn, and
Ferdinand L. Barnett

Edited by
Robert W. Rydell

University of Illinois Press

Urbana and Chicago

146011

Editor's Introduction © 1999 by the Board of Trustees
of the University of Illinois
Manufactured in the United States of America
1 2 3 4 5 C P 5 4 3 2 1

Library of Congress Cataloging-in-Publication Data
The reason why the colored American is not in the
World's Columbian Exposition : the Afro-American's
contribution to Columbian literature / Ida B.
Wells . . . [et al.] ; edited by Robert W. Rydell.
    p.   cm.
Originally published: 1893.
ISBN 0-252-02473-7 (cloth : perm. paper)
ISBN 0-252-06784-3 (papteback : perm. paper)
1. Afro-Americans—Exhibitions—History—19th
century. 2. Afro-Americans—Social conditions—
To 1964. 3. World's Columbian Exposition (1893 :
Chicago, Ill.) I. Wells-Barnett, Ida B., 1862–1931.
II. Rydell, Robert W.
E185.53.C4R43   1999
305.896073—dc21   98-58021
CIP

To

Kiki Leigh Rydell

Claire Rydell

Johanna Rydell

CONTENTS

ACKNOWLEDGMENTS

Nearly twenty years ago, when I was first beginning my research on world's fairs, I came across a copy of *The Reason Why the Colored American Is Not in the World's Columbian Exposition.* Over the years, I became convinced that students of American culture would find it interesting and important, especially if they understood its historical context. I thank Richard L. Wentworth of the University of Illinois Press for sharing this conviction and for his support. I am also grateful to the Rare Book Division of the Library of Congress for making its copy of the pamphlet available to me.

Librarians, archivists, and library staff at many institutions lent assistance to this project. I am grateful to the reference staffs at the Chicago Historical Society Library, Fisk University, Howard University, and the Schomburg Center Library for responding to my many queries. I am deeply indebted to Tammy Lau, Ronald Mahoney, and Jean Coffey in the Department of Special Collections at California State University at Fresno, George Gurney at the National Museum of American Art, Anne B. Shepherd at the Cincinnati Historical Society, and Bette Mongold and Sue Lessley at Montana State University.

My wife, Kiki Leigh Rydell, helped with the research and proofreading of this edition. I am also grateful to Theresa L. Sears and Emily Rogers for their assistance with preparing this book for publication.

David Roediger helped me round out my introduction; so did my good friends George B. Cotkin, Jonathan W. McLeod, and Billy G. Smith. Without their constructive criticism and encouragement, this project would never have been completed.

EDITOR'S INTRODUCTION

"CONTEND, CONTEND!"

ROBERT W. RYDELL

> Why are not the colored people, who constitute so large an element of
> the American population, and who have contributed so large a share to
> American greatness, more visibly present and better represented in this
> World's Exposition? —Ida B. Wells[1]

> We cut no great figure at this fair. We do not seem to be a part of it. Our
> time does not seem to be yet. When it will come no man can tell—and
> yet, I feel sure it will come though it seems like hoping against hope.
> —Frederick Douglass[2]

In 1893, Chicago hosted an international fair, the World's Columbian Exposition. This cultural spectacle, Victorian America's equiva-
lent to the modern-day Olympics and Disney World rolled into one,
occurred just twenty-eight years after the end of the Civil War, at a
moment in American history when the industrial violence of the Gilded Age made it seem as if a war between regions had been fought only
to make way for a war between social classes. No ordinary fair, the
World's Columbian Exposition was held to commemorate the 400th
anniversary of Columbus's landfall in the New World and was designed
to advance the causes of American nationalism, imperialism, and consumerism. Drawing inspiration from the great international expositions
that had been sweeping Europe since London's Crystal Palace Exhibition in 1851 and from those that had been held in the United States

beginning with the 1876 Philadelphia Centennial Exhibition, the World's Columbian Exposition put the world on display with a view toward trumpeting America's own national progress toward utopia. Some twenty million Americans visited the 1893 fair, dividing their time between the main exhibition buildings, the so-called White City, and the Midway Plaisance, the fair's amusement strip topped off with George Ferris's enormous wheel revolving 280 feet above the fairgrounds. Together with the countless millions of people who read about the fair in newspapers, magazines, and souvenir publications, fairgoers turned the World's Columbian Exposition into a cultural touchstone that they would remember for the rest of their lives.[3]

Not all of those memories were positive, however. For many African Americans, the Dream City, as the World's Columbian Exposition was sometimes known, turned into a nightmare. African Americans

"The Court of Honor, Looking West." The Court of Honor was the heart of the White City at the 1893 Chicago World's Columbian Exposition. (From Rossiter Johnson, ed., *A History of the World's Columbian Exposition,* vol. 1 [New York: D. Appleton Co., 1897], p. f486. Courtesy of the National Museum of American Art.)

were denied a voice in the fair's creation and most African-American exhibits had to be approved by all-white screening committees before they were accepted for display.[4] Equally disturbing were displays by private companies that ridiculed blacks and so-called living ethnological exhibits of "primitive" human beings that reinforced the impression among whites that blacks were closer to "savagery" than to "civilization." As the racist underpinnings of the utopia projected by the fair became clear, many African Americans concluded that the World's Columbian Exposition, with its radiant White City, had become nothing less than a Frankenstein, the cultural counterpart to the lynchings that claimed 161 African-American lives in 1892 alone.[5] If, as the sponsors of the Chicago fair proclaimed, the exposition offered a blueprint for the future course of American "civilization," then there was little doubt that this vision for the future had to be contested. The question was how.

Several prominent African Americans, including the antilynching crusader Ida B. Wells, the former slave and abolitionist Frederick Douglass, the educator Irvine Garland Penn, the lawyer and newspaper publisher Ferdinand L. Barnett, and the businessman Frederic Loudin, had an answer. They determined to publish a pamphlet that would explain, as its title indicated, *The Reason Why the Colored American Is Not in the World's Columbian Exposition*. Twenty thousand copies of the pamphlet were printed, but despite the national and, in the case of Douglass and Wells, international prominence of its authors, *The Reason Why* quickly disappeared from public notice. In part, this was because world's fair authorities and their supporters in the white press paid it no attention. But African Americans were not especially receptive to its publication either. Indeed, *The Reason Why* had the unintended effect of exacerbating divisions among blacks about how best to respond to the fair's racism. As angered as many were by the fair, some were embarrassed about having their obvious absence from the exposition called to international attention. Others questioned the strategic value of the pamphlet, wondering, in the context of the massive assault on African Americans' civil rights, if the pamphlet might not backfire and erode what little support remained among whites for social, economic, and political rights for blacks in America. Still others

"Bird's Eye View of the World's Columbian Exposition." (Hubert Howe Bancroft, *Book of the Fair*, vol. 1 [Chicago: Bancroft Co., 1893], p. 71. Courtesy of the National Museum of American Art.)

objected to the pamphlet on grounds of gender, asking whether, through her deep involvement in the pamphlet project, Ida Wells might actually be positioning herself to assume the role of national spokesperson for African Americans once the aging Frederick Douglass died.

For all these reasons—initial silence and hostility on the part of whites; initial ambivalence on the part of blacks—*The Reason Why*, until very recently, has never received its due as an important work of social and cultural criticism.[6] But now that later generations of Americans are discovering for themselves what the authors of *The Reason Why* could have told them—namely, that cultural representations matter because of their power to define social identities and to project and limit meaning—it is important to reflect on this earlier struggle that anticipated the "culture wars" characterizing American life at the close of the twentieth century. Read together and, more important, in opposition to one another, these cultural texts—one a pamphlet, the other a world's fair—underscore the cultural construction of racism in post-Reconstruction America and the struggles by African Americans for social justice in a nation that seemed determined to build its future on the basis of blueprints that featured a White City at its core.[7]

A FAIR REPRESENTATION?

When plans for the Chicago world's fair were announced in 1890, African Americans had reason for both caution and optimism. Since the end of the Civil War, the United States had held two world's fairs: the 1876 Philadelphia Centennial Exhibition and the 1884–85 New Orleans World's Industrial and Cotton Exposition. Both had demeaned African Americans but had relied on different means to achieve the same effect—namely, reducing them to second-class citizens. At the Philadelphia fair, they had been excluded from construction jobs and virtually excluded from formal participation in the fair. On the occasion of that fair's festive opening ceremonies, police had even tried to keep Frederick Douglass from taking his seat on the speakers' stand. At the New Orleans exposition, by contrast, African-American exhibits were included—in fact, materials poured into New Orleans from around the country. But these exhibits were organized into a "Colored

Department" that was effectively segregated from exhibits displayed by whites. Viewed by some blacks as a sign of progress (after all, they were represented in the fair), the Colored Department made others very uncomfortable (after all, with segregation becoming law as well as practice across the South, the Colored Department seemed to suggest that blacks were lending their tacit endorsement to this new social arrangement). As they looked forward to the Chicago fair, African Americans determined to improve on their treatment at America's earlier fairs, to press for inclusion, and to insist on equal treatment with white exhibitors. They would be disappointed on all counts.[8]

An early indication that the politics of exclusion would shape the World's Columbian Exposition came when President Benjamin Harrison, a Republican, constituted the U.S. National Commission to work with local Chicago business and political leaders in organizing the event. Harrison appointed commissioners to represent every state and territory, including sparsely populated Alaska, but failed to appoint one African American, although nearly eight million blacks were American citizens. The African-American press denounced the "simon pure and lily white" character of the commission and succeeded in pressuring Harrison to appoint a St. Louis school principal, Hale G. Parker, to serve as an alternate commissioner. Harrison's racial tokenism was blatant. More subtle, but no less apparent, was the affront of the president's decision to African-American men. In an age that prized "manliness" as one of its central virtues, African-American men were, in effect, denied the opportunity to prove their manhood in the arena where men made decisions about national affairs.[9]

That decisions about the World's Columbian Exposition would be driven by gender as well as race was clear from the outset. At the same time that it created the National Commission, the U.S. Congress, responding to the demands of white middle-class women for equal representation with men, created a separate women's board, the Board of Lady Managers, to serve as "the channel of communication through which all women or organizations of women may be brought into relation with the Exposition." Did Congress really mean "all women"? Should Congress be taken at its word? African-American women believed so. Fast on the heels of the decision by the U.S. National Commission to exclude black men from its membership, a group of African-American women active in the rapidly expanding network of black women's clubs drew up a resolution in November 1890 urging the Board of Lady Managers to agree to a separate black women's exhibit at the fair so fairgoers could "know and distinguish the exhibits and handwork of the colored women from those of the Anglo-Saxon." They further resolved that the Board of Lady Managers include a representative on the executive committee who could facilitate the inclusion of African-American exhibits in the fair.[10]

These proposals ran into two difficulties. First, the mostly affluent and all-white Board of Lady Managers, led by Bertha Honoré Palmer, wife of the Chicago real estate tycoon and hotelier Potter Palmer, proved to be unsympathetic to appeals from African-American women. Second, African-American women became increasingly divided among themselves about the wisdom of a separate exhibit.

The intransigence of the Board of Lady Managers needs to be understood in the context of the highly charged atmosphere surrounding the creation of the Woman's Building at the fair. Just when African-American women were demanding a separate exhibit within the overall women's exhibits, white women were debating whether their own displays should be integrated with the men's displays or exhibited separately. The demands by African-American women for representation on the board and for representation on the fairgrounds forced the Board of Lady Managers to face the logic of their own arguments for representation at the fair. How could some members of the board demand a separate building to represent women and, in the same breath, deny African-American women an exhibit of their own? Palmer, brilliant strategist that she was, procrastinated. She let it be known through several members of her executive committee that the board would take the concerns of African-American women under advisement, but she took no immediate action.[11]

Meanwhile, African Americans, both women and men, debated the wisdom of separate exhibits. Some, following the lead of the Chicago club woman Lettie A. Trent, believed that a separate African-American exhibit would replicate the success of the Colored Department at the New Orleans exposition by underscoring the accomplishments of blacks since Emancipation. Several prominent African Americans in New York City petitioned Congress for space in the U.S. government exhibit to display materials "pertaining to the labor-products, the moral, industrial and intellectual development of the colored people of African descent," arguing that such an exhibit would also "illustrate the growth of liberty, morality and humanity of the United States." Not all blacks agreed with the wisdom of this strategy, however. Those who followed the lead of Ferdinand L. Barnett, editor of the *Conservator*, Chicago's lone local African-American newspaper, insisted on integrating blacks' and whites' exhibits to show "we are American citizens and desire to draw no line that would tend to make us strangers in the land of our birth."[12]

Realizing that African Americans were divided, Palmer and her executive committee moved in with velvet-covered fists. Determined to play the role of conquerors, they tapped a deep reservoir of paternalism in the history of American race relations. Since most African Americans lived in the South, Palmer argued, they could and should be "virtually" represented by whites. In other words, they would have to submit exhibits through existing state committees run by whites. As a final gesture of disrespect, Palmer said she would be willing to hire an African-American clerk, an offer that further exacerbated divisions among blacks. Some argued that this position was better than nothing, while others insisted that the position was just that—nothing—because a clerk would lack the power to make decisions about exhibits. By early 1892, it was clear that African Americans would be denied collective representation at the fair and that only exhibits developed by individual blacks would be considered for display—and then, only if they met with the approval of whites.[13]

Only a few African Americans accepted the terms offered by the world's fair authorities. The sculptor Edmonia Lewis exhibited a version of her "Hiawatha" in the library of the Woman's Building. George Washington Carver, the future agricultural researcher, won honorable mention for his painting "Yucca Glorioso." The New York educator Joan Imogen Howard, the only African American to serve on a state board, compiled statistics for the New York State exhibit showing African-American achievements. In addition to these individuals, several African-American colleges organized exhibits for the Palace of Liberal Arts and Education.[14]

These were exceptions. For the most part, by the spring and summer of 1892, with the exposition opening still a year away, most African Americans had rejected the terms proffered by officials and opted not to develop exhibits for the fair. There was, of course, an enormous risk associated with this decision—namely, that whites would proceed to represent African Americans in derogatory ways intended to support the rule of white supremacy at the fair and in American society more generally.

That at least some whites were thinking in exactly these terms became clear when the R. T. Davis Milling Company, a prominent midwestern flour milling firm, persuaded Nancy Green, a fifty-seven-year-old former slave and long-time servant for a Chicago judge, to become a living advertisement at the fair for the company's self-rising Aunt Jemima Pancake Mix. Green agreed to play the part of a stereotypical plantation mammy—a role that had long been a staple of blackface minstrel shows before becoming a corporate trademark. As Aunt Jemima, Green wore a red bandanna and flipped pancakes outside the company's exhibit booth, designed in the shape of an enormous barrel of flour. While a company salesman distributed buttons that carried an Aunt Jemima image and the slogan, "I'se in town, honey," Green told nostalgic tales of plantation life to the visitors who thronged to see the show. Her performance, which became one of the hits of the fair and won a medal for her employer, was exactly the kind of role exposition directors imagined for African Americans in their dazzling White City; it also helps explain why African-American artists, educators, and inventors had so much difficulty gaining exhibition space at the World's Columbian Exposition.[15]

How should the Aunt Jemima exhibit be understood? In a sense, an argument could be made that Nancy Green succeeded where other African Americans had failed. After all, she found a gateway into the fair—right through the portals of the White City—and gained acceptance as an early icon of America's emerging culture of mass consumption that was everywhere on view at the exposition. Since no one forced her to play the part of Aunt Jemima, her role could be seen as analogous to performances by entertainers in world's fair theaters. In a fair that otherwise tended to exclude blacks, so the argument might go, the Aunt Jemima character provided a black woman the chance to be included and to gain a measure of fame—and, if not a fortune, then at least more money than she could have earned as a household servant. But as plausible as this interpretation might seem, it is important to remember that Nancy Green was not entirely free to shape her own identity. As Aunt Jemima, she is more accurately remembered, as Maurice Manring has written, as a "slave in a box," serving as the perfect—indeed, medal-winning—emblem of a fair that made the promise of easier living for whites in America's future contingent on blacks remaining in a subordinate position in U.S. society.[16]

A WAR OF POSITION

Long before the Aunt Jemima exhibit confirmed some of the worst suspicions about the motivations of the exposition sponsors, many African Americans were convinced that the World's Columbian Exposition would seal their fate as second-class citizens in the post-Reconstruction American republic. From their perspective, the exclusionary and derogatory policies of the exposition management functioned as the cultural counterparts to the assaults occurring on blacks across the South at the hands of white lynch mobs. Since the close of political Reconstruction, these ritualistic acts of murder and physical mutilation had become public spectacles often witnessed by entire communities of whites. Faced with an exponential increase in this violence against African-American men, who were often accused, without evidence, of raping white women, some African Americans began to wonder if the strategy of simply refusing to send exhibits to the Chicago world's fair sent a sufficiently strong message about the absence of social justice in the United States. If the real menace posed by the exposition lay in its capacity to bestow ideological legitimacy on the white supremacist attitudes underpinning the terrorism that had become a way of life in the South, then a stronger response was in order.

If the racist policies and messages embedded in the World's Columbian Exposition could not be changed, then the fair itself would have to be challenged. This change in strategy was initiated by three indi-viduals: Frederick Douglass, Frederic Loudin, and Ida B. Wells. Wells provided the spark.

Born into slavery in Mississippi in 1862, Wells taught school for a number of years near Memphis, Tennessee, before gaining notoriety in 1887 by suing the Chesapeake and Ohio Railroad for refusing to allow

Ida B. Wells (Department of Special Collections, University of Chicago Library)

her to sit with whites in a passenger car. She lost the suit in the state supreme court, but her experience with segregation and the southern justice system propelled her into journalism. In 1891, she helped establish an African-American newspaper in Memphis, *The Free Speech*, that gave voice to black concerns about the lack of social, economic, and political justice. These concerns crystallized in early 1892 when a white mob lynched several of her friends who had established a successful grocery business that threatened the economic security of whites. In response, Wells organized a boycott that seriously disrupted the Memphis economy. She also wrote a column that reversed the argument about the black male rapist. Referring to the eight additional lynchings that had occurred in other states during the preceding week, Wells minced few words in condemning "the same old racket." "Nobody in this section of the country believes the old threadbare lie that Negro men rape white women," she scoffed. "If Southern white men are not careful, they will over-reach themselves and public sentiment will have a reaction; a conclusion will then be reached which will be very damaging to the moral reputation of their women."[17]

By denying that African-American men were rapists and by implying, instead, that white women were responsible for seducing black men, Wells put her own life at risk. She fled to New York City, where she gained employment with the *New York Age*, one of the nation's leading African-American newspapers. She also began lecturing to African-American women's groups about "southern horrors" to raise funds for a national campaign against lynching. Her crusade attracted the attention of Frederick Douglass, who, early in the autumn of 1892, wrote to Wells from his home outside Washington, D.C.: "Brave Woman! You have done your people and mine a service which can neither be weighed nor measured. If the American conscience were only half alive . . . a scream of horror, shame and indignation would rise to Heaven."[18] What rose instead was a White City in Chicago.

Prior to meeting Wells in 1892, the aging Douglass, despondent over his son's recent death and depressed by the general apathy of whites about the plight of blacks in post–Civil War America, had accepted the invitation of the Haitian government to serve as that nation's official representative at the Chicago fair—an invitation that had been issued to honor Douglass's service as the American minister to Haiti between 1889 and 1891.[19] The timing of the invitation was exquisite. Just when Chicago's exposition authorities thought they had effectively excluded African Americans from their fair, America's best-known African American found a port of entry under the auspices of a foreign country long remembered for the slave insurrection led by Toussaint-Louverture.

In late October, acting in his official capacity as Haiti's representative, Douglass traveled to Chicago for week-long ceremonies marking the dedication of the World's Columbian Exposition. Once in Chicago, he came to appreciate, like never before, the full meaning of the fair. These ceremonies, he quickly understood, were being held not only to dedicate a fair but to rededicate a nation so recently torn asunder by civil war. What Douglass saw were spectacular buildings nearing completion, parades stretching for miles, and formal ceremonies that served

Frederick Douglass (Prints and Photographs Division, Library of Congress)

as the occasion for introducing the Pledge of Allegiance into the nation's schools.[20] No doubt Douglass, like other African Americans, was pleased, as Barnett's *Conservator* put it, that "the colored people were not entirely ignored in the dedication exercises of the world's fair." But their presence was minimal. True, African-American soldiers marched in the military parades and African-American children helped form a "living American flag" outside the U.S. Government Building. Douglass himself appeared at various exposition events, including the high-society ball, and "was greeted with rounds of applause."[21] Yet, as gratifying as these tokens of appreciation may have been, they were just that—tokens that could not atone for the larger injustices of lynching and of denying African Americans full representation at the fair itself. As Douglass put it: "The presence of one of this race in a prominent position would speak more for the moral civilization of the American republic than all the domes, towers and turrets of the magnificent buildings that adorn the Exposition grounds."[22]

Having seen the future being mapped out in Chicago, Douglass returned to Washington, D.C., determined to change it. He found a willing ally in the person of Ida B. Wells. In the autumn of 1892, shortly before Wells received an invitation to carry her antilynching crusade to England, Douglass and Wells linked arms across generations and gender divisions and determined to publish a pamphlet that would challenge the legitimacy of the White City and explain to the world why African Americans were not represented at the Chicago world's fair.

This was a heady and daunting proposition. For one thing, the pamphlet would cost money. For another, with the fair scheduled to open on 1 May, time was short. For yet another, the pamphlet would run the risk of further alienating those few remaining whites who sympathized with blacks' demands for social justice. After all, it was abundantly clear that the 1893 fair was white America's show. It promised to loop together Victorian-era political and cultural "correctness" into an epoch-defining spectacle about the meaning of Civilization and Culture—both with a capital C. Criticism of this nationalizing construct, as America's cultural authorities at national and local levels made clear, would be about as welcome as a hard freeze in June.

Raising money for oppositional political causes is not easy now; in the 1890s, it was nearly an impossible task for Wells and Douglass, given the general level of poverty among African Americans. Douglass, however, had connections, among them Frederic J. Loudin, shoe manufacturer, inventor, and manager of the Fisk Jubilee Singers. Loudin evidently had heard Wells lecture in Washington, D.C., and learned that Douglass had proposed "laying before the world at the Columbian Exposition, in painting and print, the outrages to which we are subjected in this 'land of the free'(?)." Inspired by Wells and Douglass, and enraged by lynchings in the South, especially by a particularly brutal one in Paris, Texas, and by the racist policies of the fair, Loudin wrote an open letter to Douglass demanding action: "Let us compile the accounts of the lynchings, the shootings, the flaying alive, the torture, the burning at the stake and all the other kindred horrors of this christian(?) people and print in book or pamphlet form for free distribution at the great Exposition, and lay the whole matter bare before the world in all its hideousness." He promised to put cash on the line— "at least $50.00," no small sum in 1892—to launch the project.[23]

That was music to Wells's and Douglass's ears. With Wells preparing for an April departure for England, Douglass proceeded to issue a fund-raising appeal for the pamphlet project in the form of a public circular tellingly entitled "To the Friends of Equal Rights":

WHEREAS, the 400th anniversary of the discovery of America by Christopher Columbus is soon to be celebrated in Chicago by the World's Fair Columbian Exposition;

WHEREAS, the absence of colored people from participating therein will be construed to their disadvantage by the representatives of the civilized world there assembled;

THEREFORE, the undersigned, in obedience to a request that we take under consideration the matter of setting ourselves right before the world, recommend:

1st That a carefully prepared pamphlet, setting forth the past and present condition of our people and their relation to American civilization be printed in English, German, French and Spanish.

2nd That these pamphlets be distributed free during all the months of the World's Columbian Exposition.[24]

F. J. Loudin (center), with the Fisk Jubilee Singers (Department of Special Collections, Fisk University Library)

Wells and Douglass convinced themselves that there would be widespread support for their appeal. They would be proved wrong.

Avoiding a Train Wreck

The first source of opposition originated early in 1893 with an alliance between World's Columbian Exposition authorities and a handful of Boston-area African-American ministers and women's club organizers who proposed setting aside 25 August as "Colored People's Day" at the fair. In one sense, this proposal appeared to be an extension of the fair's policy of setting aside special days at the fair for white ethnic groups. But in another sense, it represented a calculated effort to win over a few influential blacks who had been insisting on having a day at the fair to demonstrate African-American cultural achievements since Emancipation. By acquiescing in these demands, exposition authorities could maintain the fiction that they were being inclusive and, at the same time, portray their critics as inveterate complainers.[25]

Wells immediately understood what exposition officials were trying to accomplish. Like Albion Tourgée, one of her few supporters in the white press, she believed that "to make the 'colored people's day' a day of 'glorious jubilee' will be to certify to the world that the colored people of the United States are content with the treatment accorded them as citizens of the great Republic in the several states of the American Union." When the *Indianapolis Freeman,* one of the leading black newspapers, denounced the plan in a stinging editorial headlined "No 'Nigger Day' Wanted," Wells wrote the newspaper a congratulatory letter. But her volley in support of the *Freeman* backfired.[26]

In the midst of the uproar about Jubilee Day, the *Freeman* received notice of Wells's and Douglass's plans to produce a pamphlet. It wasted no time likening this scheme to Jubilee Day and, in an editorial titled "No 'Nigger Day,' No 'Nigger Pamphlet!'" argued that the pamphlet, like Jubilee Day, would only humiliate African Americans in the eyes of the world.[27]

That headline deeply offended Douglass. With Wells on her way to England, Douglass responded to the *Freeman* in no uncertain terms: "Why may we not tell of our persecution and murder in this country because of our race and color? Shall our tongues be mute and our pens paralyzed because our words may pain the ears of our oppressors and shame them? . . . No brother *Freeman,* we must not be silent. We have but one weapon unimpaired and that weapon is speech, and not to use this and use it freely, is treason to the oppressed." In reply, the *Freeman* reiterated its earlier condemnation of Douglass. Two weeks later, Douglass wrote again to the *Freeman*'s editor, conceding that "with your opposition it is not likely that money will be raised to publish the pamphlet."[28]

Indeed, with the fund-raising effort seemingly dead in the water and with Wells on her way to a distant shore, Douglass evidently began having doubts about the pamphlet project. Whether he shared his doubts with Wells is uncertain, but it is clear that he determined to pursue a different tactic. When Boston supporters of the Jubilee Day initiative issued a circular promoting their plans, Douglass's name appeared prominently on the masthead listing supporters of their cause.[29]

Why was Douglass drawn to the Jubilee Day proposal? In the first place, he believed that the history of African Americans made clear that "all that we have ever received has come to us in small concessions and it is not the part of wisdom to despise the day of small things."[30] "Making do" would become the phrase a later generation of cultural theorists would coin to describe exactly what Douglass was reasoning in 1893.[31] But there was more to Douglass's thinking than merely accepting "the day of small things." He found Jubilee Day appealing because it was in accord with his own thinking about how to use his position as Haiti's representative at the fair to advance the cause of African Americans. By providing a vehicle for inserting African-American cultural representations into the fair, Jubilee Day could serve as a cultural weapon, a veritable Trojan horse, or so it seemed to Douglass, that would enable blacks to combat the racism of the fair from within its gates. Like the pamphlet, Jubilee Day would advance the cause of social justice. But unlike the pamphlet, Jubilee Day would permit African Americans to penetrate the White City and critique it from within.

When Wells returned in June from her series of antilynching lectures in England, she traveled directly to Chicago, where she expected to meet with Douglass to discuss the progress that had been made on the pamphlet. Instead, as she recounts in her autobiography, she learned that Douglass was ready to abandon the project in favor of devoting his time and energy to organizing the Jubilee Day festivities. With the fair "in full blast" and Douglass on the verge of backing out of the project, Wells held his feet to the fire. Would he agree to support the pamphlet scheme if she could raise the money? Douglass agreed and Wells proceeded to gather "the representative women of Chicago together and," as she later recalled, "asked their help in arranging a series of Sunday afternoon meetings at the different churches—Mr. Douglass to preside and I to speak. These women worked enthusiastically, and as a result we had crowded meetings at Bethel, Quinn Chapel, St. Stephen, and other churches." The results were impressive. "In this way," Wells noted, "we raised the needed five hundred dollars quickly, which added to the fifty dollars each which had been pledged by Mr. Douglass and Mr. Loudin, enabled us to print a creditable little book called *The Reason Why the Colored American Is Not in the World's Columbian Exposition.*"[32]

Wells was absolutely right to credit Chicago-area women with raising the necessary money for the pamphlet. They were still enraged over their earlier treatment by the Board of Lady Managers and had just reiterated their anger at a session of the Congress of Representative Women that was one of dozens of congresses held in conjunction with the fair that summer. "In this Congress," declared Fannie Barrier Williams, the wife of a leading Chicago African-American lawyer, "we ask to be known and recognized for what we are worth. If it be the high purpose of these deliberations to lessen the resistance to woman's progress, you can not fail to be interested in our struggles against the many oppositions that harrass us. . . . Women of the dominant race can not afford to be responsible for the wrongs we suffer, since those who do injustice can not escape a certain penalty."[33] When Wells and Douglass appealed for funds to these women, who had fought so hard for African-American representation at the fair, many were only too happy to contribute to the cause of making *The Reason Why* available at no charge, except for three cents to cover the cost of postage.

Though the results of their appeal for funds were impressive, the process had been more contentious than Wells remembered. Many leading African-American newspapers kept up their barrage of criticism of the pamphlet idea. Douglass continued to support the Jubilee Day celebration. With the *Freeman* leading the charge, critics in the press highlighted differences between Wells and Douglass. Earlier that spring, the *Freeman* had delighted in noting that Wells and Douglass were at odds over Jubilee Day and had gleefully forecast "that both the 'Pamphlet' and 'Jubilee' ideas are dead already."[34] But this was simply wishful thinking on the *Freeman's* part. In fact, Wells and Douglass had agreed to disagree about the best strategy to pursue. Wells held fast to her "oppositional" mode of thinking, her militant refusal to compromise her principles, while Douglass increasingly steered in the direction of supporting an "alternative" stance toward the fair, believing that it would be better to work within the existing structure than to challenge its very existence.[35] Still, their relationship became increasingly strained as Douglass devoted his time and energy to arranging Jubilee Day and Wells concentrated her energies on the pamphlet. In mid-July, the train wreck that the *Freeman* anticipated almost occurred.

To attract African Americans to the fair on Jubilee Day, exposition officials, claiming to be responding to the requests of some blacks, announced that free watermelon stands would be set up on the fairgrounds. The *Freeman* exploded in rage: "The Board of Directors have furnished the day, some members of the race have pledged to furnish the 'niggers,' (in our presence Negroes), and if some thoughtful and philanthropic white man is willing to furnish watermelons, why should he be gibbeted?" The *Freeman* urged African Americans to boycott Jubilee Day.[36]

So did Ida Wells. In a letter to the Cleveland *Gazette*, she asked that the "good Lord forgive those fool Afro-Americans in the east who would ridicule and humiliate our people, not only before the eyes of the people of this country, but before those of the whole world." She added that "the Colored Men's Protective Association" had recently held its national meeting in Chicago and "declined the invitation of the world's fair directors to accept August 25 as 'Colored Folks' Day.'"[37]

Douglass held his temper and refrained from attacking Wells in public, knowing full well that a collision with Wells would play into the divide-and-conquer strategy of exposition officials. He became increasingly discouraged about the Jubilee Day prospects but held fast to his commitment to showcase the talents of several young African-American writers and musicians, including the poet Paul Laurence Dunbar, whom Douglass employed in the Haitian Building, and the violin prodigy Will Marion Cook, who had studied with the Czech composer Antonín Dvořák.[38]

Wells also met discouragement and frustration as she worked to publish the pamphlet. Most African-American newspapers continued to ridicule the pamphlet idea. True, she had raised enough money to offset some of the printing costs, but not enough to subsidize publication entirely. So when *The Reason Why* was finally published on 30 August 1893, Wells had to abandon plans to publish it in several European languages. She had only enough money to bring out an English-language edition with short prefaces in French and German.

Then, in a final twist of irony, the flames of controversy that Wells helped to fan over Jubilee Day dominated the African-American press and overshadowed news of the pamphlet's publication.[39]

Feelings of anticipation and dread mixed in about equal proportion as Jubilee Day dawned—and not just for Douglass and Wells. For the better part of eight months, African Americans had debated the merits of this "special day." They had also debated the wisdom of attending the fair, period. While there appears to have been no overt discrimination against black visitors, the fair's discriminatory employment practices doubtless caused many to have second thoughts about attending. Now, with the Aunt Jemima show in full swing and the prospect of watermelon stands being set up on the fairgrounds, the question had become whether a boycott of Jubilee Day would be an effective means of protest. No one knew for sure what the answer would be.[40]

When Douglass arrived at the fairgrounds, his heart surely sank when he saw the watermelon stands going up. Just two months earlier, he had written his daughter: "If I could I would treat [my grandchildren] to a visit to the world's fair." Now he knew that one of the most important performers, the singer Sissieretta Jones, had decided to support the boycott, as had Chicago's African-American clergy. Perhaps his critics had been right and Jubilee Day had been a mistake. The white press was having a field day. "To-day," one newspaper snidely observed, "our colored friends are enjoying themselves at Jackson Park and this is believed to be the last of the dark days at the fair."[41] But Douglass determined to go through with the afternoon ceremonies at Festival Hall, one of the White City's main buildings.

When Douglass arrived for the ceremonies, a small crowd, numbering between 1,000 and 2,500 people, about two-thirds of them African Americans, had assembled. To remind the audience of a time, not that long before, when at least some whites had worked with black abolitionists to hasten the end of slavery, Douglass walked to the platform in the company of Isabella Beecher-Hooker, sister of Harriet Beecher Stowe, the author of *Uncle Tom's Cabin.* As they proceeded to their seats, a newspaper reported, "the applause was deafening." But as Douglass began his speech, which he called "The Race Problem in America," several white hecklers disrupted his remarks with "jeers and catcalls." Douglass momentarily faltered, but he had faced hostile whites before. According to Dunbar, who sat nearby waiting to read his poem "The Colored American," Douglass found his voice and sounded like the abolitionist of old: "Full, rich and deep came the sonorous tones, compelling attention, drowning out the catcalls as an organ would a penny whistle." What Douglass said was sharp and to the point:

> Men talk of the Negro problem. There is no Negro problem. The problem is whether the American people have honesty enough, loyalty enough, honor enough, patriotism enough to live up to their own Constitution. . . . During the war we were eyes to your blind, legs to your lame, shelter to the shelterless among your sons. Have you forgotten that now? Today we number 8,000,000 people. Today a desperate effort is being made to blacken the character of the Negro and to brand him as a moral monster. In fourteen States of this Union wild mobs have taken the place of law. They hang, shoot, burn men of race without justice and without right. Today the Negro is barred out of almost every reputable and decent employment. We only ask to be treated as well as you treat the late enemies of your national life. We love this country and we want that you should treat us as well as you do those who love only a part of it. . . . Look at the progress the Negro has made in thirty years. We have come up out of Dahomey unto this. Measure the Negro. But not by the standard of the splendid civilization of the Caucasian. Bend down and measure him—measure him from the depths out of which he has risen.

This was an eloquent speech, but Douglass's strategy for challenging the White City was flawed.[42]

Pushed to the wall by the racism of dominant society, Douglass attempted to trump the race card by playing a card of his own—one drawn from the deck dealt by his opponents. To counter arguments that African Americans were not as "civilized" as whites, he tapped into the assumptions of evolutionary anthropology as presented at the fair and invited comparisons between African Americans and Africans, hoping to persuade his audience that the former were more "civilized" than the latter. Whether he realized it or not, his argument had the effect of fueling dominant stereotypes of Africans, who were put on display in the Dahomeyan Village at the end of the Midway Plaisance as exemplars of "savagery." These stereotypes, in turn, were routinely used by whites—especially white cartoonists—to debase African Americans.[43]

The *Indianapolis Freeman* pronounced Jubilee Day a "dismal failure," but not everyone shared this judgment. Ida Wells, for one, saw matters differently. She followed through on her intentions to boycott Jubilee Day, but after reading newspaper accounts of Douglass's speech, she recalled being "so swelled with pride over his masterly presentation of our case that I went straight out to the fair and begged his pardon for presuming in my youth and inexperience to criticize him for an effort which had done more to bring our cause to the attention of the American people than anything else which had happened during the fair." Douglass graciously accepted Wells's apology and later wrote to a friend: "I regard Miss Wells as a brave and truthful woman devoted to the cause of her outraged and bitterly persecuted people."[44]

AFTERMATH

Douglass and Wells mended fences but had little time to reflect on what had transpired. In less than a week they were scheduled to participate in the international Labor Congress held in conjunction with the fair and to contribute to a session devoted to "negro labor" in the South. As Douglass and Wells saw it, this event, which attracted labor leaders and social reformers from around the world, presented another opportunity for them to press their case for social justice.[45]

What they could not have anticipated was how the session on black labor in the South would help propel another African American to national prominence. He was Booker T. Washington, the young and relatively unknown principal of the Tuskegee Institute. Invited to address the Labor Congress by its organizer, the social critic Henry Demarest Lloyd, Washington saw race relations in very different terms than Douglass and Wells. "Whatever else may be said against the South," he declared, "there is this in its favor: that when it comes to business pure and simple and to the exercise of skilled labor, the South accords to the black man almost the same rights that it does to the

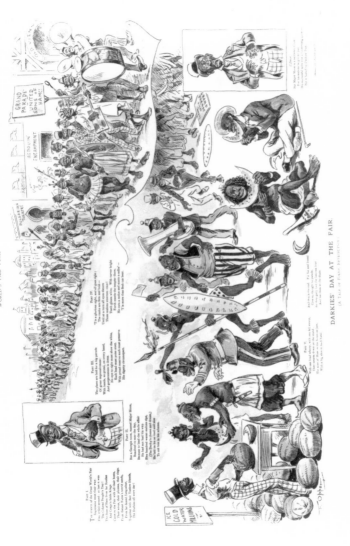

"Darkies' Day at the Fair (A Tale of Poetic Retribution)." (*World's Fair Puck* 16 [21 August 1893]: 186–87. Courtesy of the National Museum of American Art.)

Darkies' Day at the Fair (A Tale of Poetic Retribution)

PART I

The Events of the Great World's Fair
Impressive went their way.
Time rolled around; at last it was
The Colored People's Day!
The Sons of Ham from far Soudan
And Congo's Sable Kings
Came to the Fair with all the hosts,
Their wives, their plumes, their rings.
From distant Nubia's torrid sands,
From far-famed Zanguebar,
Together with their Yankee Friends,
The Darkies all were dar!

PART II

But a Georgia coon, named Major
  Moon,
Resolved to mar the day,
Because to lead the whole affair
He had not his way.
Five hundred water-melon ripe,

(The Darky's theme and dream,)
He laid on ice so cold and nice
To aid him in his scheme.

PART III

The plans are laid for a big parade
Of great impressiveness;
With bands, so grand, on every hand,
And gorgeousness in dress.
No eye to right must show the white,
Each head must poise erect
With proud reserve each must
  preserve
His dignity circumspect.

PART IV

'T is a glorious sight, all goes right;
  the ranks are firm and bold—
Until at a turn all eyes discern
Those melons DRIPPING COLD!
Teeth gleamed white. With carver bright

Forth stands the tempter there.
He cuts a melon and starts a-sellin'—
'T is more than flesh can bear.

PART V

With one loud whoop, with one fell
  swoop,
They swarm down on the stand;
The sons of Ham in the foremost jam,
With a big slice in each hand.
And this is the end. For foe and friend
Give no thought to parade.
As they gaily loot the luscious fruit
And hie them to the shade.

L'ENVOI

But Major Moon is a saddened Coon
For his melons he got no pay.
His successful spite was a boomerang
  quite—
But it busted up Darkies' Day.

white man." Washington added: "I believe that when we come right down to it the colored mechanic has a better chance in the South than in the North. . . . All the Negro asks of the world of labor is a fair chance." He also emphasized his belief "that this friction between the races is to pass away as the black man gets hold of the things the white man wants and respects, like the trades and mechanic arts. It is along

Booker T. Washington (Prints and Photographs Division, Library of Congress)

this line we are to find the solution of all these problems in the South, and on this line they are slowly but surely being solved."[46] Conciliation, not agitation, was the gist of Washington's message, and with it he threatened to pull the rug right out from under Douglass and Wells.

Wells retorted to Washington's assertions by wondering why, if what Washington said was true, "the colored people never seemed to get out of debt." The answer, she argued, was clear: the "Southern white men did not want to lose the colored population so long as the latter would consent to remain laborers, for the negro to-day was the greatest wealth-producing factor in the South." Douglass, who chaired the session, echoed Wells's criticism. To the Tuskegee principal's claim that African Americans could find economic solutions based on self-help to the problems confronting them in the South, Douglass replied: "The laborer in the South was not only a victim of the mortgage system, but also a victim of a script system that was equally vicious. The man who in slavery days said to the negro, 'You shall be a slave or die,' now added, 'You shall work for me at the wages I propose or starve.'"[47]

Douglass and Wells offered informed rebuttals, but they did not discredit Washington. His remarks at the Labor Congress came to the attention of a group of Atlanta business and political leaders who were dreaming of organizing a world's fair in their city in 1895. After learning of Washington's address, Atlanta's civic leaders invited him to help sell their plans for a fair to the U.S. Congress. In return, they agreed to allow Washington to deliver an opening-day speech at the fair and to permit African Americans to organize a separate "Negro Building" for their exhibits. Washington's speech, variously called the "Atlanta Compromise Address" or the "Atlanta Exposition Address," became one of the most famous in American history, remembered both for his tacit acceptance of segregation and for his arguments against political agitation to secure improved conditions for African Americans.[48]

There was no small measure of irony in the fact that, despite all the energy invested by Wells and Douglass, the World's Columbian Exposition actually served to advance the cause of Washington's accommodationist program. Yet it is also important to recall that memories of the White City, far from immobilizing Wells, led her to redouble her fight for civil rights and social justice.

After Douglass's death in 1895, African Americans were divided about the best course of action to pursue to redress their grievances. These divisions would be reflected in the future careers of the other two authors who contributed to *The Reason Why*.[49]

Ferdinand L. Barnett, who had initially led the opposition to plans for a segregated African-American exhibit at the 1893 fair, supported Wells. Indeed, they fell in love and married in 1895. While Ida B. Wells-

Ferdinand L. Barnett (Department of Special Collections, University of Chicago Library)

Barnett continued to lead the antilynching campaign, Barnett devoted his life to the study and practice of civil rights law. Together, Wells, who died in 1931, and Barnett, who died in 1936, lived lives that Douglass had urged in his introduction to *The Reason Why* when he wrote: "Contend, contend!"[50]

Irvine Garland Penn veered into Booker T. Washington's camp. In 1895, the directors of the Atlanta fair hired Penn to take charge of the "Negro Department" at the exposition. He turned the so-called Negro Building at the fair into a showcase of industrial education that lent visible support to Washington's accommodationist philosophy. Following the Atlanta fair, Penn preached the gospel of self-help from his increasingly important positions in educational and religious institutions. In 1912, he moved his family to Cincinnati, where he became renowned for his fund-raising activities on behalf of African-American educational institutions. He died in 1930 from injuries apparently sustained at the hands of whites while he was traveling on a passenger train.[51]

READING *The Reason Why*

There are many reasons to read *The Reason Why*, with its "proud, ironic," and barbed subtitle, *The Afro-American's Contribution to Columbian Literature.*[52] First, it sheds light on the socioeconomic and political reality of African-American life a century ago. Second, it provides insight into the different strategies that African Americans developed to counter the racism embedded in a cultural event that functioned as an engine of American nationalism. Third, it also makes clear that struggles over cultural representation, at the close of the twentieth century, are nothing new in American life.

The pamphlet's preface, addressed "To the Seeker after Truth," establishes the tone. Authored by Wells, it frames the issues clearly: "The wealth created by [African-American] industry has afforded to the white people of this country the leisure essential to their great progress in education, art, science, industry and invention." Given their contributions to "American prosperity and civilization," Wells asks, "why are not the colored people, who constitute so large an element of the

Irvine Garland Penn and Family (Cincinnati Historical Society)

American population, and who have contributed so large a share to American greatness, more visibly present and better represented in this World's Exposition?"

Douglass reemphasizes the point, noting the "flagrant contradiction" between the ideals of the World's Columbian Exposition and the actual treatment of African Americans by exposition authorities and the dominant society. Would that it were possible to tell the world, Douglass sardonically muses, "that this World's Columbian Exposition, with its splendid display of wealth and power, its triumphs of art and its multitudinous architectural and other attractions, is a fair indication of the elevated and liberal sentiment of the American people, and that to the colored people of America, morally speaking, the World's Fair now in progress, is not a whited sepulcher." He insists that "all this, and more, we would gladly say of American laws, manners, customs and Christianity. But unhappily, nothing of all this can be said, without qualification and without flagrant disregard of the truth." So, when all is said and done, the White City was indeed a "whited sepulcher," a reliquary of American civilization.[53]

Why were African Americans so enraged about being excluded from this fair? Because the racism at the World's Columbian Exposition mirrored, framed, and reinforced the larger horrors confronting blacks throughout the United States where white supremacy meant segregation, second-class citizenship, and sometimes lynching. Unlike Douglass, who couched his contribution to *The Reason Why* in moral terms, Wells insisted that racism in all of its various guises should also be understood in political and economic terms. In essays entitled "Class Legislation," "The Convict Lease System," and "Lynch Law," she argues that disfranchisement, convict labor, and lynching were not just moral issues but vehicles for maintaining the imbalance of wealth and power in the South. To these forces legally and physically restraining African Americans from making progress was now added another, cultural threat—the White City.

What if African Americans had been allowed to organize their own displays for the 1893 fair? Some hints of what that exhibit might have looked like are evident in the title of Penn's essay, "The Progress of the Afro-American since Emancipation." Had it been organized, the exhibit may well have fallen into the categories that Penn developed as subheadings for his article and featured the enormous achievements African Americans had made in education as well as their patents, works of art, and musical accomplishments—all of these made within a system of racial apartheid that had been constructed to take the place of slavery.

But only a few of these accomplishments were actually on display at the fair. "Theoretically open to all Americans," Barnett explains, "the Exposition practically is, literally and figuratively, a 'White City,' in the building of which the Colored American was allowed no helping hand, and in its glorious success he has no share." The *reason why*, Barnett continues, is clear: from start to finish, the fair was "color proof"; it was consciously designed to exclude African Americans from management positions and from employment on the fairgrounds. After detailing the struggles of blacks to gain inclusion in the fair, Barnett concludes by reminding his readers of Douglass's appointment as Haiti's commissioner to the fair and by emphasizing the reality that "the Colored American received from a foreign power the place denied to him at home." With this final sentence, Barnett makes clear that African Americans had not given up on their struggle for social justice and would continue to seek support at home and abroad.

There is still another reason for reading *The Reason Why*—namely, it makes clear that, for all of its considerable power to sustain and perpetuate white supremacist values, the World's Columbian Exposition was never so absolute that it crushed popular resistance and the efforts by people in positions of relative powerlessness to secure control over their own cultural representations. Confronted by derogatory and exclusionary practices of the White City, Wells, Douglass, Penn, and Barnett determined to script their own representation of African-American culture in the form of an anti-exhibitionary pamphlet, their "contribution to Columbian Literature." In so doing, they challenged the moral authority of the White City and condemned those who embraced its racially exclusive roadmap to America's future.

A Note on the Text

In her note "To the Public," dated 30 August 1893, on the back cover of *The Reason Why* (see p. 82), Wells calls attention to the rush to get the pamphlet printed, probably in an effort to have it ready by Jubilee Day on 25 August. The haste—better understood as urgency—with which the pamphlet was printed is apparent in its inconsistent capitalization and punctuation practices. I have silently corrected the most obvious printer's errors, primarily mistakes in capitalization and where periods instead of commas were inserted into sentences. But I have not reedited the pamphlet in its entirety to make it conform to late twentieth-century rules of American English usage. To do so would have diluted the sense of urgency that inspired both the writing and the printing of *The Reason Why*.

Very few copies of the pamphlet have survived. This edition was prepared from the copy that is part of the Susan B. Anthony Collection in the Rare Book Division of the Library of Congress.

NOTES

1. See p. 4.

2. Frederick Douglass to [Rosetta Sprague?], 20 June 1893, Frederick Douglass Papers, correspondence, microfilm reel 32, Library of Congress, Washington, D.C. (cited hereafter as Douglass Papers).

3. There is a great deal of literature about the 1893 fair. A relatively accessible contemporary history of the fair is Hubert Howe Bancroft, *The Book of the Fair*, 2 vols. (New York, 1894). Other primary sources, including Bancroft's volumes, are readily available on microfilm in *The Books of the Fairs*, a collection produced by Research Publications, Inc., in 1992.

There is a large secondary literature about the 1893 fair and a growing number of studies of other fairs. Two useful introductions are: *The Books of the Fairs: Materials about World's Fairs, 1834–1916, in the Smithsonian Institution Libraries* (Chicago, 1993) and John Findling and Kimberly Pelle, *Historical Dictionary of World's Fairs* (New York, 1990). See also Robert W. Rydell, *All the World's a Fair: Visions of Empire at American International Expositions, 1876–1916* (Chicago, 1984). On the Chicago fair, see Rodney Reid Badger, *The Great American Fair: The World's Columbian Exposition and American Culture* (Chicago, 1979); Alan Trachtenberg, *The Incorporation of America: Culture and Society in the Gilded Age* (New York, 1982), chap. 7; Neil Harris, Wim de Wit, James Gilbert, and Robert W. Rydell, *Grand Illusions: Chicago's World's Fair of 1893* (Chicago, 1993); and Robert Muccigrosso, *Celebrating the New World: Chicago's World's Columbian Exposition of 1893* (Chicago, 1993).

4. Studies of the controversy surrounding African Americans in the fair include: Elliott Rudwick and August Meier, "Black Man in the 'White City': Negroes and the Columbian Exposition, 1893," *Phylon* 26 (1965): 354–61; Ann Massa, "Black Women in the White City," *Journal of American Studies* 8 (1974):

319–37; Dreck Spurlock Wilson, "Black Involvement in Chicago's Previous World's Fairs," manuscript, 1984, vertical files, Chicago Historical Society, Chicago, Ill.; Gail Bederman, *Manliness and Civilization: A Cultural History of Gender and Race in the United States, 1880–1917* (Chicago, 1995); and Anna R. Paddon and Sally Turner, "African Americans and the World's Columbian Exposition," *Illinois Historical Journal* 88 (1995): 19–36.

5. A poem published in a special Exposition issue of *The Bulletin of Atlanta University* asks readers to "pause, when like a Frankenstein, / A nation dares create another race" (48 [July 1893]: 1). On the history of lynching in the American South, see *Under Sentence of Death,* ed. W. Fitzhugh Brundage (Chapel Hill, N.C., 1997).

6. *The Selected Works of Ida B. Wells-Barnett* (New York, 1991), and the selections reproduced in Mildred I. Thompson, *Ida B. Wells-Barnett* (Brooklyn, 1990), are important acts of cultural recovery.

7. Bederman, *Manliness and Civilization,* 40, notes how the pamphlet "revised the hegemonic civilization discourse."

8. For an account of earlier fairs, see Rydell, *All the World's a Fair,* chaps. 1, 3.

9. Rudwick and Meier, "Black Man," 354–55; Bederman, *Manliness and Civilization,* 31–44.

10. Massa, "Black Women," provides the best account of these developments.

11. Ibid. For the controversy about white women's role in the fair, see Jeanne Madeline Weimann, *The Fair Women* (Chicago, 1981); Frances K. Pohl, "Historical Reality or Utopian Ideal?" *International Journal of Women's Studies* 5 (1982): 289–311; and Mary Cordato, "Representing the Expansion of Woman's Sphere: Women's Work and Culture at the World's Fairs of 1876, 1893, and 1904" (Ph.D. diss., New York University, 1989).

12. Barnett and his supporters quoted in Women's Columbian Association, *Aim and Plan of Action* (Chicago, 1891), cited in Massa, "Black Women," 323; Wynell Burroughs Schamel and Richard A. Blondo, "Petition for a Fair Representation of African Americans at the World's Columbian Exposition," *Social Education* 56.6 (1992): 349–52. See also "The Afro-American Annex to the World's Fair," *New York Age,* 14 March 1891; "No Separate Exhibit," ibid., 23 May 1891.

13. Massa, "Black Women," 326–33.

14. Wilson, "Black Involvement," 10. See also *Report of the Board of General Managers of the Exhibit of the State of New York at the World's Columbian Exposition* (Albany, N.Y., 1894), 176–77.

15. Maurice M. Manring, *Slave in a Box: The Strange Career of Aunt Jemima* (Charlottesville, Va., 1998), 72–78.

16. Ibid. On black reactions to the culture of consumerism, see Carl Pedersen, "Black Responses to Consumption: From Frederick Douglass to Booker T. Washington," in *Consumption and American Culture,* ed. David E. Nye and Carl Pedersen (Amsterdam, 1991), 194–203.

17. The starting point for learning about Ida B. Wells-Barnett is her autobiography, *Crusade for Justice: The Autobiography of Ida B. Wells,* ed. Alfreda Duster (Chicago, 1970). This should be supplemented with the following studies: Thomas C. Holt, "The Lonely Warrior: Ida B. Wells-Barnett and the Struggle for Black Leadership," in *Black Leaders of the Twentieth Century,* ed. John Hope Franklin and August Meier (Urbana, Ill., 1982), 39–50; Mildred Thompson, "Ida B. Wells-Barnett: An Exploratory Study of an American Black Woman, 1893–1930" (Ph.D. diss., George Washington University, 1979); Hazel V. Carby, "'On the Threshold of Woman's Era': Lynching, Empire, and Sexuality in Black Feminist Theory," in *"Race," Writing, and Difference,* ed. Henry Louis Gates Jr. (Chicago, 1985), 301–16; idem, *Reconstructing Womanhood: The Emergence of the Afro-American Woman Novelist* (New York, 1987), 108–16; Karen Malinda Mason, "Testing the Boundaries: Women, Politics, and Gender Roles in Chicago, 1890–1930" (Ph.D. diss., University of Michigan, 1991); and Patricia Ann Schecter, "'To Tell the Truth Freely': Ida B. Wells and the Politics of Race, Gender, and Reform in America, 1880–1913" (Ph.D. diss., Princeton University, 1993).

18. Douglass to Wells, 25 Oct. 1892, in Wells, *Southern Horrors* (New York, 1892), preface.

19. There is an extensive literature about Frederick Douglass. The best starting point is William McFeeley's *Frederick Douglass* (New York, 1991), whose chapter on Douglass's involvement with the Chicago fair is excellent.

20. On the Pledge of Allegiance and the fair, see John T. Rodgers, "Authorship of the Pledge of Allegiance to the Flag: A Report," Legislative Reference Service, July 18, 1957, Library of Congress, Washington, D.C.

21. Chicago *Conservator* quoted in "At the World's Fair," Detroit *Plaindealer,* 4 November 1892.

22. Frederick Douglass, "Inauguration of the World's Columbian Exposition," *World's Columbian Exposition Illustrated* 3.1 (March 1893): 300.

23. F. J. Loudin, "A World's Fair Suggestion," Detroit *Plaindealer,* 24 February 1893. In an editorial of 16 December 1892, the *Plaindealer* had encouraged African Americans to insist on an exhibit that would illustrate "how judge

lynch operates in the free land of ours." See also Douglass to Loudin, 6 March 1893, reel 7, Douglass Papers. One of Loudin's inventions, a window lock, is advertised in the broadside "Loudin's Original Fisk Jubilee Singers: After a Six Years Tour around the World," in the John Hay Library, Providence, R.I.

24. "To the Friends of Equal Rights," unidentified newspaper clipping, n.d., reel 3, Douglass Papers.

25. Rudwick and Meier, "Black Man," 359–60.

26. Tourgée quoted in "That 'Jubilee Day,'" *Indianapolis Freeman*, 18 March 1893; "No 'Nigger Day' Wanted," ibid., 25 February 1893; "Miss Well's [*sic*] Congratulations," ibid., 4 March 1893.

27. "No 'Nigger Day,' No 'Nigger Pamphlet,'" ibid., 25 March 1893.

28. "Hon. Frederick Douglass Writes the *Freeman* a Letter Defending the Pamphlet Idea—Editorial Comment," ibid., 8 April 1893; "Another Letter from Mr. Douglass," ibid., 15 April 1893; Douglass to W. Allison Sweeney, 8 April 1893, reel 7, Douglass Papers. The *Freeman* was not alone in condemning the pamphlet idea. See also "World's Fair Appeal" and "Gone Abroad," Washington, D.C., *Bee*, 15 April 1893. In the latter article, the *Bee* ridiculed Wells for going to England: "What will now become of that pamphlet? O! Miss Wells how could you leave your people so suddenly? What is to become of the world's fair pamphlet, which is to disclose so many important facts?"

29. "World's Fair Columbian Exposition," circular, [1893], reel 13, Douglass Papers.

30. "Another Letter from Mr. Douglass," *Indianapolis Freeman*, 15 April 1893.

31. See, for instance, Michel de Certeau, *The Practice of Everyday Life* (Berkeley, Calif., 1984).

32. Wells-Barnett, *Crusade for Justice*, 116–17.

33. *The World's Congress of Representative Women*, vol. 2, ed. May Wright Sewall (Chicago, 1894), 710.

34. "Another Letter from Mr. Douglass," *Indianapolis Freeman*, 15 April 1893.

35. The distinction between alternative and oppositional modes of thinking and action is drawn by Raymond Williams, *Problems in Materialism and Culture* (London, 1980), 40.

36. "The Jubilee Day Folly," *Indianapolis Freeman*, 12 August 1893.

37. "Miss Ida B. Wells," Cleveland *Gazette*, 22 July 1893. See also "Afro-Americans at the Fair," Topeka *Weekly Call*, 15 July 1893.

38. McFeeley, *Frederick Douglass*, 370–71. Cook and Dunbar first met at the fair and subsequently collaborated in producing several so-called coon songs,

carved out of the tradition of blackface minstrelsy, that became the rage among white audiences at the turn of the century. See Will Marion Cook, "Writings by Will Marion Cook—Paul Dunbar Notes," n.d., Mercer Cook Papers, Howard University, Washington, D.C. The influence of the 1893 fair on the emergence of the "coon song" genre deserves further study; a useful starting point is James H. Dormon, "Shaping the Popular Image of Post-Reconstruction American Blacks: The 'Coon Song' Phenomenon of the Gilded Age," *American Quarterly* 40 (1988): 450–71. The influence of the fair on ragtime has been noted by David Guion, "From Yankee Doodle Thro' to Handel's Largo: Music at the World's Columbian Exposition," *College Music Symposium* 24 (Spring 1989): 81–96.

39. "Douglass' Wasted Zeal," *Indianapolis Freeman,* 5 August 1893, continued the *Freeman's* attack on Douglass and Wells. For a brief, favorable review of the pamphlet, see Cleveland *Gazette,* 23 September 1893.

40. Rudwick and Meier, "Black Man," 357.

41. Douglass to [Rosetta Sprague?], 20 June 1893, reel 32, Douglass Papers; "Negroes at the Fair," Chicago *Evening Post*[?], clipping, World's Columbian Exposition Scrapbooks, vol. 32, Chicago Historical Society, Chicago, Ill.

42. For accounts of Jubilee Day, see McFeeley, *Frederick Douglass,* 370–71; Rudwick and Meier, "Black Man," 359–61; "The World in Min[i]ature," *Indianapolis Freeman,* 2 September 1893; and "Honor to the Race," Topeka *Weekly Call,* 9 September 1893. See also "Big Day for the Negro," *Chicago Times,* 26 August 1893; "Honor to Their Race," Chicago *Inter-Ocean,* 26 August 1893— all in World's Columbian Exposition Scrapbooks, vol. 32, Chicago Historical Society, Chicago, Ill.

43. Douglass had given a speech on the occasion of the opening of the Dahomeyan Village in which he "praised their dance and ceremonies, which, he remarked, were all on the same principle, if not quite so well developed, as those of people living nearer to civilization." See "Opening of the Dahoman [*sic*] Village," *Chicago Tribune,* 30 May 1893. For an insightful analysis of the cartoons, see Manon Niquette and William J. Buxton, "Meet Me at the Fair: Sociability and Reflexivity in Nineteenth-Century World Expositions," *Canadian Journal of Communication* 22 (1997): 81–113.

44. "The World in Min[i]ature"; Wells-Barnett, *Crusade for Justice,* 118–19; Douglass to R. A. Armstrong, 22 May 1894, Frederick Douglass file, Schomburg Center Library.

45. See Dennis B. Downey, "The Congress on Labor at the 1893 World's Columbian Exposition," *Illinois State Historical Society Journal* 76 (1983): 131–38.

46. "An Account of a Speech before the Labor Congress, Chicago [2 Sep-

tember 1893]," in *Booker T. Washington Papers,* ed. Louis R. Harlan, vol. 3 (Urbana, Ill., 1974), 364–66. One should compare this account from the Chicago *Inter-Ocean* with "Color Line in Labor," Chicago *Sunday Herald* [?], World's Columbian Exposition Scrapbooks, vol. 33, Chicago Historical Society, Chicago, Ill.

47. "Color Line in Labor."

48. On the "Atlanta Compromise Address," see Rydell, *All the World's a Fair,* 82–85.

49. On the leadership crisis, see Holt, "Lonely Warrior."

50. Biographical information on Barnett is scanty. See Harold F. Gosnell, *Negro Politicians* (Chicago, 1935), 85; *Bench and Bar of Chicago* (Chicago [?], n.d.), 419.

51. Information about Penn's life is from Joanne K. Abrams, "Irvine Garland Penn: A Pioneer in Afro-American Progress," manuscript (Howard University, 1973), Cincinnati Historical Society, Cincinnati, Ohio.

52. Massa, "Black Women," 336, calls attention to the subtitle's significance.

53. In a surviving fragment of what might be a draft for his introduction, Douglass's language is more exact. He says the fair is "a whited sepulcher fair without and full of dead men's bones within." See "World's Columbian Exposition Fragment,", n.d., reel 19, Douglass Papers.

Frederick Douglass.

THE REASON WHY

The Colored American is not
in the World's Colum-
bian Exposition.

Susan B. Anthony
Rochester
N. Y.

Jan. 11, 1903

The Afro-American's Contribution to Columbian Literature

Copies sent to any address on receipt of three cents for
postage. Address MISS IDA B. WELLS, 128
S. Clark Street, Chicago, Ill., U. S. A

Pamphlet cover with signature of American feminist leader Susan B. Anthony. The name "Frederick Douglass" was probably pencilled in by a librarian at the time the Library of Congress acquired the pamphlet.

PREFACE

To the Seeker after Truth

Columbia has bidden the civilized world to join with her in celebrating the four-hundredth anniversary of the discovery of America,
and the invitation has been accepted. At Jackson Park are displayed exhibits of her natural resources, and her progress in the arts and sciences.
But that which would best illustrate her moral grandeur has been ignored.

The exhibit of the progress made by a race in 25 years of freedom
as against 250 years of slavery, would have been the greatest tribute to
the greatness and progressiveness of American institutions which could
have been shown the world. The colored people of this great Republic
number eight millions—more than one-tenth the whole population of
the United States. They were among the earliest settlers of this continent, landing at Jamestown, Virginia in 1619 in a slave ship, before the
Puritans, who landed at Plymouth in 1620. They have contributed a
large share to American prosperity and civilization. The labor of one-
half of this country has always been, and is still being done by them.
The first credit this country had in its commerce with foreign nations
was created by productions resulting from their labor. The wealth created by their industry has afforded to the white people of this country

the leisure essential to their great progress in education, art, science, industry and invention.

Those visitors to the World's Columbian Exposition who know these facts, especially foreigners will naturally ask: Why are not the colored people, who constitute so large an element of the American population, and who have contributed so large a share to American greatness, more visibly present and better represented in this World's Exposition? Why are they not taking part in this glorious celebration of the four-hundredth anniversary of the discovery of their country? Are they so dull and stupid as to feel no interest in this great event? It is to answer these questions and supply as far as possible our lack of representation at the Exposition that the Afro-American has published this volume.

A Tout Chercheur de Verité

L'Amérique a convié le monde civilisé à se joindre à elle pour célébrer le quatre-centième anniversaire de la découverte de l'Amérique, et son invitation a été acceptée.

Certes, le parc Jackson fait largement connaitre ses ressources naturelles et ses progrès dans les arts et dans les sciences; mais on a oublié justement ce qui devait donner le plus d'éclat à son élévation morale.

En mettant en effet sous les yeux les progrès qu'a faits en 25 ans de liberté une race sortant d'un esclavage de 250 ans, on eût rendu à la grandeur et au développement des institutions américaines le tribut le plus beau que pourrait voir le monde. Les gens de couleur de cette grande République sont au nombre de huit millions, plus du dix-septième de la population totale des Etats-Unis. Ils ont été parmi les plus anciens colons de ce continent, arrivant à Jamestown, Virginie, en 1619 dans un canot d'esclave avant les Puritans qui débarquèrent à Plymouth en 1620. Ils ont contribué dans une large mesure à la prospérité et à la civilisation de l'Amérique. Ce sont eux qui ont accompli et accomplissent encore la moitié du travail de ce pays; c'est le produit, le résultat de leur travail qui a été la base du premier crédit que son commerce a obtenu de l'étranger. Si la race blanche a pu prendre son temps pour les grands progrès auxquels elle est parvenue dans l'éducation, dans les sciences, dans les arts, dans l'industrie et dans les inventions, c'est aux ressources créées par leur labeur qu'elle le doit.

Les visiteurs de l'Exposition universelle colombienne qui sont au courant de ces faits, les étrangers surtout, vont naturellement demander: Pourquoi donc la classe de couleur, qui constitue un élément si considérable de la population américaine, et qui a si largement contribué à la grandeur de l'Amérique n'est-elle pas mieux répresentée et ne paraît-elle pas plus visiblement dans cette Exposition? Pourquoi ces hommes ne prennent-ils point part à cette glorieuse célébration du quatre-centième anniversaire de la Découverte de leur pays? Sont ils donc d'une incapacité et d'une stupidité telles qu'ils ne sentent aucun intérêt pour eux dans ce grand évènement? C'est pour répondre à ces questions et suppléer autant que possible à notre oubli de représentation à l'Exposition que la race noire d'Amérique a publié ce livre.

AN ALLE, DIE WAHRHEIT SUCHEN

Columbus hat die civilisirte Welt eingeladen, sich an der vierhundertjährigen Feier der Entdeckung Amerika's zu betheiligen; diese Einladung ist angenommen worden. Im Jackson-Park befinden sich Ausstellungsgegenstände, die von seinem Naturreichthum zeugen, von dem Fortschritte in Kunst und Wissenschaft, während indessen Eines, das seine moralische Größe am besten bezeugen würde, vollständig außer Acht gelassen worden ist.

Die Darstellung des Fortschrittes gemacht von einer Rasse während fünfundzwanzigjähriger Freiheit, gegenüber dem einer zweihundertundfünfzigjährigen Sklaverei, würde den besten Beweis für die Größe, und den Fortschritt Amerika's geliefert haben. Die farbige Bevölkerung dieser großen Republik beläuft sich auf acht Millionen—mehr als ein Zehntel der Gesammtbevölkerung der Vereinigten Staaten. Die Farbigen waren unter den frühesten Ansiedlern dieses Continents, da sie bereits im Jahre 1619 in Jamestown, Virginien landeten und zwar als Sklaven, noch ehe die Puritaner ihr Erscheinen machten, die in 1620 landeten. Sie haben einen beträchtlichen Theil für das allgemeine Wohl und Civilisation beigetragen; die Hälfte der Arbeit des ganzen Landes wurde und wird jetzt noch von ihnen verrichtet. Das Produkt, durch welches Amerika im Verkehr mit den übrigen Nationen zuerst Bedeutung gewonnen, war erzeugt durch ihre Arbeit. Der durch ihren Fleiß erzeugte Reichthum hat der weißen Bevölkerung die Muße gegeben, die zu einem Fortschritte auf den Gebieten der Bildung, Kunst und Wissenschaft, Industrie und Erfindung nöthig ist.

Jene Besucher der Weltausstellung, welchen diese Thatsachen bekannt sind und vorzüglich Fremde werden natürlich fragen: Warum sind die Farbigen, die einen so bedeutenden Theil der amerikanischen Bevölkerung ausmachen und so viel zur Größe Amerika's beigetragen haben, nicht besser auf der Ausstellung vertreten? Warum betheiligen sie sich nicht an der vierhundertjährigen Feier der Entdeckung ihres Landes? Sind sie so beschränkt und unwissend, daß sie kein Interesse an diesem wichtigen Ereigniß nehmen? Es ist mit Hinsicht auf die Antwort zu diesen Fragen und auf eine bessere Vertretung auf der Ausstellung, daß der Afrikanisch-Amerikaner den vorliegenden Band veröffentlicht.

CHAPTER I

INTRODUCTION

By Frederick Douglass

The colored people of America are not indifferent to the good opinion of the world, and we have made every effort to improve our first years of freedom and citizenship. We earnestly desired to show some results of our first thirty years of acknowledged manhood and womanhood. Wherein we have failed, it has been not our fault but our misfortune, and it is sincerely hoped that this brief story, not only of our successes, but of trials and failures, our hopes and disappointments will relieve us of the charge of indifference and indolence. We have deemed it only a duty to ourselves, to make plain what might otherwise be misunderstood and misconstrued concerning us. To do this we must begin with slavery. The duty undertaken is far from a welcome one.

It involves the necessity of plain speaking of wrongs and outrages endured, and of rights withheld, and withheld in flagrant contradiction to boasted American Republican liberty and civilization. It is always more agreeable to speak well of one's country and its institutions than to speak otherwise; to tell of their good qualities rather than of their evil ones.

There are many good things concerning our country and countrymen of which we would be glad to tell in this pamphlet, if we could do so, and at the same time tell the truth. We would like for instance to tell our visitors that the moral progress of the American people has kept even pace with their enterprise and their material civilization; that practice by the ruling class has gone on hand in hand with American professions; that two hundred and sixty years of progress and enlightenment have banished barbarism and race hate from the United States; that the old things of slavery have entirely passed away, and that all things pertaining to the colored people have become new; that American liberty is now the undisputed possession of all the American people; that American law is now the shield alike of black and white; that the spirit of slavery and class domination has no longer any lurking place in any part of this country; that the statement of human rights contained in its glorious Declaration of Independence, including the right to life, liberty and the pursuit of happiness is not an empty boast nor a mere rhetorical flourish, but a soberly and honestly accepted truth, to be carried out in good faith; that the American Church and clergy, as a whole, stand for the sentiment of universal human brotherhood and that its Christianity is without partiality and without hypocrisy; that the souls of Negroes are held to be as precious in the sight of God, as are the souls of white men; that duty to the heathen at home is as fully recognized and as sacredly discharged as is duty to the heathen abroad; that no man on account of his color, race or condition, is deprived of life, liberty or property without due process of law; that mobs are not allowed to supercede courts of law or usurp the place of government; that here Negroes are not tortured, shot, hanged or burned to death, merely on suspicion of crime and without ever seeing a judge, a jury or advocate; that the American Government is in reality a Government of the people, by the people and for the people, and for all the people; that the National Government is not a rope of sand, but has both the power and the disposition to protect the lives and liberties of American citizens of whatever color, at home, not less than abroad; that it will send its men-of-war to chastise the murder of its citizens in New Orleans or in any other part of the south, as readily as for the same purpose it will send them to Chili, Hayti or San Domingo; that our national sovereignty, in its rights to protect the lives of American citizens is ample and superior to any right or power possessed by the individual states; that the people of the United States are a nation in fact as well as in name; that in time of peace as in time of war, allegiance to the nation is held to be superior to any fancied allegiance to individual states; that allegiance and protection are here held to be reciprocal; that there is on the statute books of the nation no law for the protection of personal or political rights, which the nation may not or can not enforce, with or without the consent of individual states; that this World's Columbian Exposition, with its splendid display of wealth and power, its triumphs of art and its multitudinous architectural and other attractions, is a fair indication of the elevated and liberal sentiment of the American people, and that to the colored people of America, morally speaking, the World's Fair now in progress, is not a whited sepulcher.

All this, and more, we would gladly say of American laws, manners, customs and Christianity. But unhappily, nothing of all this can be said, without qualification and without flagrant disregard of the truth. The explanation is this: We have long had in this country, a system of iniquity which possessed the power of blinding the moral perception, stifling the voice of conscience, blunting all human sensibilities and perverting the plainest teaching of the religion we have here professed, a system which John Wesley truly characterized as the sum of all villanies, and one in view of which Thomas Jefferson, himself a slaveholder, said he "trembled for his country" when he reflected "that God is just and that His justice cannot sleep forever." That system was American slavery. Though it is now gone, its asserted spirit remains.

The writer of the initial chapter of this pamphlet, having himself been a slave, knows the slave system both on the inside and outside. Having studied its effects not only upon the slave and upon the master, but also upon the people and institutions by which it has been surrounded, he may therefore, without presumption, assume to bear witness to its baneful influence upon all concerned, and especially to its malign agency in explaining the present condition of the colored people of the United States, who were its victims; and to the sentiment held toward them both by the people who held them in slavery, and the people of the country who tolerated and permitted their enslavement, and the bearing it has upon the relation which we the colored people sustain to the World's Fair. What the legal and actual condition of the colored people was previous to emancipation is easily told.

It should be remembered by all who would entertain just views and arrive at a fair estimate of our character, our attainments and our worth in the scale of civilization, that prior to the slave-holders' rebellion thirty years ago, our legal condition was simply that of dumb brutes. We were classed as goods and chattels, and numbered on our masters' ledgers with horses, sheep and swine. We were subject to barter and sale, and could be bequeathed and inherited by will, like real estate or any other property. In the language of the law: A slave was one in the power of his master to whom he belonged. He could acquire nothing, have nothing, own nothing that did not belong to his master. His time and talents, his mind and muscle, his body and soul, were the property of the master. He, with all that could be predicated of him as a human being, was simply the property of his master. He was a marketable commodity. His money value was regulated like any other article; it was increased or diminished according to his perfections or imperfections as a beast of burden.

Chief Justice Taney truly described the condition of our people when he said in the infamous Dred Scott decision that they were supposed to have no rights which white men were bound to respect. White men could shoot, hang, burn, whip and starve them to death with impunity. They were made to feel themselves as outside the pale of all civil and political institutions. The master's power over them was complete and absolute. They could decide no question of pursuit or condition for themselves. Their children had no parents, their mothers had no husbands and there was no marriage in a legal sense.

But I need not elaborate the legal and practical definition of slavery. What I have aimed to do, has not only been to show the moral depths, darkness and destitution from which we are still emerging, but to explain the grounds of the prejudice, hate and contempt in which we are still held by the people, who for more than two hundred years doomed us to this cruel and degrading condition. So when it is asked why we are excluded from the World's Columbian Exposition, the answer is Slavery.

Outrages upon the Negro in this country will be narrated in these pages. They will seem too shocking for belief. This doubt is creditable to human nature, and yet in view of the education and training of those who inflict the wrongs complained of, and the past condition of those upon whom they were inflicted as already described, such outrages are not only credible but entirely consistent and logical. Why should not these outrages be inflicted?

The life of a Negro slave was never held sacred in the estimation of the people of that section of the country in the time of slavery, and the abolition of slavery against the will of the enslavers did not render a slave's life more sacred. Such a one could be branded with hot irons, loaded with chains, and whipped to death with impunity when a slave. It only needed be said that he or she was impudent or insolent to a white man, to excuse or justify the killing of him or her. The people of the south are with few exceptions but slightly improved in their sentiments towards those they once held as slaves. The mass of them are the same to-day that they were in the time of slavery, except perhaps that now they think they can murder with a decided advantage in point of economy. In the time of slavery if a Negro was killed, the owner sustained a loss of property. Now he is not restrained by any fear of such loss.

The crime of insolence for which the Negro was formerly killed and for which his killing was justified, is as easily pleaded in excuse now, as it was in the old time and what is worse, it is sufficient to make the charge of insolence to provoke the knife or bullet. This done, it is only necessary to say in the newspapers, that this dead Negro was impudent and about to raise an insurrection and kill all the white people, or that a white woman was insulted by a Negro, to lull the conscience of the north into indifference and reconcile its people to such murder. No proof of guilt is required. It is enough to accuse, to condemn and punish the accused with death. When he is dead and silent, and the murderer is alive and at large, he has it all his own way. He can tell any story he may please and will be believed. The popular ear is open to him, and his justification is sure. At the bar of public opinion in this country all presumptions are against the Negro accused of crime.

The crime to which the Negro is now said to be so generally and specially addicted, is one of which he has been heretofore, seldom accused or supposed to be guilty. The importance of this fact cannot be over estimated. He was formerly accused of petty thefts, called a chicken thief and the like, but seldom or never was he accused of the atrocious crime of feloniously assaulting white women. If we may believe his accusers this is a new development. In slaveholding times no one heard of any such crime by a Negro. During all the war, when there was the fullest and safest opportunity for such assaults, nobody ever heard of such being made by him. Thousands of white women were left for years in charge of Negroes, while their fathers, brothers and husbands were absent fighting the battles of the rebellion; yet there was no assault upon such women by Negroes, and no accusation of such assault. It is only since the Negro has become a citizen and a voter that this charge has been made. It has come along with the pretended and baseless fear of Negro supremacy. It is an effort to divest the Negro of his friends by giving him a revolting and hateful reputation. Those who do this would make the world believe that freedom has changed the whole character of the Negro, and made of him a moral monster.

This is a conclusion revolting alike to common sense and common experience. Besides there is good reason to suspect a political motive for the charge. A motive other than the one they would have the world believe. It comes in close connection with the effort now being made to disfranchise the colored man. It comes from men who regard it innocent to lie, and who are unworthy of belief where the Negro is concerned. It comes from men who count it no crime to falsify the returns of the ballot box and cheat the Negro of his lawful vote. It comes from those who would smooth the way for the Negro's disfranchisement in clear defiance of the constitution they have sworn to support—men who are perjured before God and man.

We do not deny that there are bad Negroes in this country capable of committing this, or any other crime that other men can or do commit. There are bad black men as there are bad white men, south, north and everywhere else, but when such criminals, or alleged criminals are found, we demand that their guilt shall be established by due course of law. When this will be done, the voice of the colored people everywhere will then be "Let no guilty man escape." The man in the South who says he is for Lynch Law because he honestly believes that the courts of that section are likely to be too merciful to the Negro charged with this crime, either does not know the South, or is fit for prison or an insane asylum.

Not less absurd is the pretense of these law breakers that the resort to Lynch Law is made because they do not wish the shocking details of the crime made known. Instead of a jury of twelve men to decently try the case, they assemble a mob of five hundred men and boys and circulate the story of the alleged outrage with all its concomitant, disgusting detail. If they desire to give such crimes the widest publicity they could adopt no course better calculated to secure that end than by a resort to lynch law. But this pretended delicacy is manifestly all a sham, and the members of the blood-thirsty mob bent upon murder know it to be such. It may deceive people outside of the sunny south, but not those who know as we do the bold and open defiance of every sentiment of modesty and chastity practiced for centuries on the slave plantations by this same old master class.

We know we shall be censured for the publication of this volume. The time for its publication will be thought to be ill chosen. America is just now, as never before, posing before the world as a highly liberal and civilized nation, and in many important respects she has a right to this reputation. She has brought to her shores and given welcome to a greater variety of mankind than were ever assembled in one place since the day of Pentecost. Japanese, Javanese, Soudanese, Chinese, Cingalese, Syrians, Persians, Tunisians, Algerians, Egyptians, East Indians, Laplanders, Esquimoux, and as if to shame the Negro, the Dahomians are also here to exhibit the Negro as a repulsive savage.

It must be admitted that, to outward seeming, the colored people of the United States have lost ground and have met with increased and galling resistance since the war of the rebellion. It is well to understand this phase of the situation. Considering the important services rendered by them in suppressing the late rebellion and the saving of the Union, they were for a time generally regarded with a sentiment of gratitude by their loyal white fellow citizens. This sentiment however, very naturally became weaker as, in the course of events, those services were retired from view and the memory of them became dimmed by time and also by the restoration of friendship between the north and the south. Thus, what the colored people gained by the war they have partly lost by peace.

Military necessity had much to do with requiring their services during the war, and their ready and favorable response to that requirement was so simple, generous and patriotic, that the loyal states readily adopted important amendments to the constitution in their favor. They accorded them freedom and endowed them with citizenship and the right to vote and the right to be voted for. These rights are now a part of the organic law of the land, and as such, stand to-day on the national statute book. But the spirit and purpose of these have been in a measure defeated by state legislation and by judicial decisions. It has nevertheless been found impossible to defeat them entirely and to relegate colored citizens to their former condition. They are still free.

The ground held by them to-day is vastly in advance of that they occupied before the war, and it may be safely predicted that they will not only hold this ground, but that they will regain in the end much of that which they seem to have lost in the reaction. As to the increased resistance met with by them of late, let us use a little philosophy. It is easy to account in a hopeful way for this reaction and even to regard it as a favorable symptom. It is a proof that the Negro is not standing still. He is not dead, but alive and active. He is not drifting with the current, but manfully resisting it and fighting his way to better conditions than those of the past, and better than those which popular opinion prescribes for him. He is not contented with his surroundings, but nobly dares to break away from them and hew out a way of safety and happiness for himself in defiance of all opposing forces.

A ship rotting at anchor meets with no resistance, but when she sets sail on the sea, she has to buffet opposing billows. The enemies of the Negro see that he is making progress and they naturally wish to stop him and keep him in just what they consider his proper place.

They have said to him "you are a poor Negro, be poor still," and "you are an ignorant Negro, be ignorant still and we will not antagonize you or hurt you." But the Negro has said a decided no to all this, and is now by industry, economy and education wisely raising himself to conditions of civilization and comparative well being beyond anything formerly thought possible for him. Hence, a new determination is born to keep him down. There is nothing strange or alarming about this. Such aspirations as his when cherished by the lowly are always resented by those who have already reached the top. They who aspire to higher grades than those fixed for them by society are scouted and scorned as upstarts for their presumptions.

In their passage from an humble to a higher position, the white man in some measure, goes through the same ordeal. This is in accordance with the nature of things. It is simply an incident of a transitional condition. It is not the fault of the Negro, but the weakness, we might say the depravity, of human nature. Society resents the pretentions of those it considers upstarts. The new comers always have to go through with this sort of resistance. The old and established are ever adverse to the new and aspiring. But the upstarts of to-day are the elite of tomorrow. There is no stopping any people from earnestly endeavoring to rise. Resistance ceases when the prosperity of the rising class becomes pronounced and permanent.

The Negro is just now under the operation of this law of society. If he were white as the driven snow, and had been enslaved as we had been, he would have to submit to this same law in his progress upward. What the Negro has to do then, is to cultivate a courageous and cheerful spirit, use philosophy and exercise patience. He must embrace every avenue open to him for the acquisition of wealth. He must educate his children and build up a character for industry, economy, intelligence and virtue. Next to victory is the glory and happiness of manfully contending for it. Therefore, contend! contend!

That we should have to contend and strive for what is freely conceded to other citizens without effort or demand may indeed be a hardship, but there is compensation here as elsewhere. Contest is itself enobling. A life devoid of purpose and earnest effort, is a worthless life. Conflict is better than stagnation. It is bad to be a slave, but worse to be a willing and contented slave. We are men and our aim is perfect manhood, to be men among men. Our situation demands faith in ourselves, faith in the power of truth, faith in work and faith in the influence of manly character. Let the truth be told, let the light be turned on ignorance and prejudice, let lawless violence and murder be exposed.

The Americans are a great and magnanimous people and this great exposition adds greatly to their honor and renown, but in the pride of their success they have cause for repentance as well as complaisance, and for shame as well as for glory, and hence we send forth this volume to be read of all men.

CHAPTER II

CLASS LEGISLATION

[By Ida B. Wells]

The Civil War of 1861–5 ended slavery. It left us free, but it also left us homeless, penniless, ignorant, nameless and friendless. Life is derived from the earth and the American Government is thought to be more humane than the Russian. Russia's liberated serf was given three acres of land and agricultural implements with which to begin his career of liberty and independence. But to us no foot of land nor implement was given. We were turned loose to starvation, destitution and death. So desperate was our condition that some of our statesmen declared it useless to try to save us by legislation as we were doomed to extinction.

The original fourteen slaves which the Dutch ship landed at Jamestown, Virginia in 1619, had increased to four millions by 1865, and were mostly in the southern states. We were liberated not only empty-handed but left in the power of a people who resented our emancipation as an act of unjust punishment to them. They were therefore armed with a motive for doing everything in their power to render our freedom a curse rather than a blessing. In the halls of National legislation the Negro was made a free man and citizen. The southern states, which had seceded from the Union before the war, regained their autonomy by accepting these amendments and promising to support the constitution. Since "reconstruction" these amendments have been largely nullified in the south, and the Negro vote reduced from a majority to a cipher. This has been accomplished by political massacres, by midnight outrages of Ku Klux Klans, and by state legislative enactment. That the legislation of the white south is hostile to the interests of our race is shown by the existence in most of the southern states of the convict lease system, the chain-gang, vagrant laws, election frauds, keeping back laborers' wages, paying for work in worthless script instead of lawful money, refusing to sell land to Negroes and the many political massacres where hundreds of black men were murdered for the crime(?) of casting the ballot. These were some of the means resorted to during our first years of liberty to defeat the little beneficence comprehended in the act of our emancipation.

The South is enjoying to-day the results of this course pursued for the first fifteen years of our freedom. The Solid South means that the South is a unit for white supremacy, and that the Negro is practically disfranchised through intimidation. The large Negro population of that section gives the South thirty-nine more votes in the National Electoral College which elects the President of the United States, than she would otherwise have. These votes are cast by white men who represent the Democratic Party, while the Negro vote has heretofore represented the entire Republican Party of the South. Every National Congress has thirty-nine more white members from the South in the House of Representatives than there would be, were it not for the existence of her voiceless and unrepresented Negro vote and population. One Representative is allowed to every 150,000 persons. What other States have usurped, Mississippi made in 1892, a part of her organic law.

The net result of the registration under the educational and poll tax provision of the new Mississippi Constitution is as follows.

	Over 21 years.	Registered votes.
Whites - - -	110,100	68,127
Negroes - -	147,205	8,615
Total - - -	257,305	76,742

In 1880 there were 130,278 colored voters, a colored majority of 22,024. Every county in Mississippi now has a white majority. Thirty-three counties have less than 100 Negro votes.

Yazoo county, with 6,000 Negroes of voting age, has only nine registered votes, or one to each 666. Noxubee has four colored voters or one to each 150 colored men. In Lowndes there is one colored voter to each 310 men. In the southern tier counties on the Gulf about one Negro man in eight or ten is registered, which is the best average.

Depriving the Negro of his vote leaves the entire political, legislative, executive and judicial machinery of the country in the hands of the white people. The religious, moral and financial forces of the country are also theirs. This power has been used to pass laws forbidding intermarriage between the races, thus fostering immorality. The union, which the law forbids, goes on without its sanction in dishonorable alliances.

Sec. 3291, M.& V.Code Tennessee, provides that: The intermarriage of white persons with Negroes, Mulattoes or persons of mixed blood descended from a Negro to the third generation inclusive, or their living together as man and wife in this State, is hereby forbidden.

Sec. 3292, M. & V. Code, Tenn., provides that: The persons knowingly violating the provisions in above Section shall be deemed guilty of a felony, and upon conviction thereof shall undergo imprisonment in the penitentiary not less than one nor more than five years; and the court may, in the event of conviction, on the recommendation of the jury, substitute in lieu of punishment in the penitentiary, fine and imprisonment in the county jail.

NOTES:—It need not charge the act to have been done knowingly. Such persons may be indicted for living together as man and wife though married in another state where such marriages are lawful. 7 Bok. 9. This law is constitutional. 3 Hill's 287.

Out of 44 states only twenty-three states and territories allow whites and Negroes to marry if they see fit to contract such alliances, viz: Louisiana, Illinois, Kansas, Connecticut, Iowa, Maine, Massachusetts, Michigan, Minnesota, Montana, New Hampshire, New Jersey, New York, North Dakota, Ohio, Oklahoma, Pennsylvania, Rhode Island, South Dakota, Vermont, Washington, Wisconsin, and Wyoming. All of these are northern states and territories except one—Louisiana.

The others, especially Virginia, Maryland, W. Virginia, Delaware, North Carolina, South Carolina, Georgia, Florida, Alabama, Mississippi, Arkansas, Kentucky, Missouri, Indiana, Tennessee, and Texas, have laws similar to the Tennessee Statute. Under these laws men and women are prosecuted and punished in the courts of these states for inter-marrying, but not for unholy alliances.

"The Thirteenth amendment to the Constitution making the race citizens, was virtually made null and void by the legislatures of the reconstructed states. So it became necessary to pass the Civil Rights Bill giving colored people the right to enter public places and ride on first-class railroad cars."—Johnson's History of the Negro race in America. This Bill passed Congress in 1875. For nearly ten years it was the Negro's only protection in the south. In 1884 the United States Supreme Court declared the Civil Rights Bill unconstitutional. With "state's rights" doctrine once more supreme and this last barrier removed, the southern states are enacting separate car laws. Mississippi, Louisiana, Texas, Arkansas, Tennessee, Alabama, Georgia and Kentucky have each passed a law making it punishable by fine and imprisonment for colored persons to ride in the same railway carriage with white persons unless as servants to white passengers. These laws have all been passed within the past 6 years. Kentucky passed this law last year (1892). The legislatures of Missouri, West Virginia and North Carolina had such bills under consideration at the sessions this year, but they were defeated.

Aside from the inconsistency of class legislation in this country, the cars for colored persons are rarely equal in point of accommodation. Usually one-half the smoking car is reserved for the "colored car." Many times only a cloth curtain or partition run half way up, divides this "colored car" from the smoke, obscene language and foul air of the smokers' end of the coach. Into this "separate but equal(?)" half-carriage are crowded all classes and conditions of Negro humanity, without regard to sex, standing, good breeding, or ability to pay for better accommodation. White men pass through these "colored cars" and ride in them whenever they feel inclined to do so, but no colored woman however refined, well educated or well dressed may ride in the ladies, or first-class coach, in any of these states unless she is a nurse-maid traveling with a white child. The railroad fare is exactly the same in all cases however. There is no redress at the hands of the law. The men who execute the law share the same prejudices as those who made these laws, and the courts rule in favor of the law. A colored young school teacher was dragged out of the only ladies coach on the train in Tennessee by the conductor and two trainmen. She entered suit in the state courts as directed by the United States Supreme Court. The Supreme Court of the State of Tennessee, although the lower courts had awarded damages to the plaintiff, reversed the decision of those courts and ruled that the smoking car into which the railway employees tried to force the plaintiff was a first-class car, equal in every respect to the one in which she was seated, and as she was violating the law, she was not entitled to damages.

The Tennessee law is as follows,

——Chapter 52——Page 135—An Act to promote the comfort of passengers on railroad trains by regulating separate accommodations for the white and colored races.

SECTION 1. Be it enacted by the General Assembly of the State of Tennessee—That all railroads carrying passengers in the State (other than street railroads) shall provide equal but separate accommodations for the white and colored races, by providing two or more passenger cars for each passenger train, or by dividing the passenger cars by a partition so as to secure separate accommodations; PROVIDED, that any person may be permitted to take a nurse in the car or compartment set aside for such persons; PROVIDED, that this Act shall not apply to mixed and freight trains which only carry one passenger or combination passenger and baggage; PROVIDED, always that in such cases the one passenger car so carried shall be partitioned into apartments, one apartment for the whites and one for the colored.

SEC. 2. Be it further enacted: That the conductors of such passenger trains shall have power and are hereby required to assign to the car or compartments of the car (when it is divided by a partition) used for the race to which such passengers belong, and should any passenger refuse to occupy the car to which he or she is assigned by such conductor, said conductor shall have power to refuse to carry such passenger on his train, and for such neither he nor the railroad company shall be liable for any damages in any court in this State.

SEC. 3. Be it further enacted: That all railroad companies that shall fail, refuse or neglect to comply with the requirements of section 1, of this Act shall be deemed guilty of a misdemeanor, and, upon conviction in a court of competent jurisdiction, be fined not less than one hundred, nor more than four hundred dollars, and any conductor that shall fail, neglect or refuse to carry out the provisions of this Act shall, upon conviction, be fined not less than twenty-five, nor more than fifty dollars for each offense.

SEC. 4. Be it further enacted: That this Act take effect ninety days from and after its passage, the public welfare requiring it.

Passed March 11, 1891.

Thomas R. Myers.
Speaker of the House of Representatives.

Approved March 27, 1891.

W. C. DISMUKES,
Speaker of Senate.

JOHN P. BUCHANAN,
Governor.

CHAPTER III

THE CONVICT LEASE SYSTEM

The Convict Lease System and Lynch Law are twin infamies which flourish hand in hand in many of the United States. They are the two great outgrowths and results of the class legislation under which our people suffer to-day. Alabama, Arkansas, Florida, Georgia, Kentucky, Louisiana, Mississippi, Nebraska, North Carolina, South Carolina, Tennessee and Washington claim to be too poor to maintain state convicts within prison walls. Hence the convicts are leased out to work for railway contractors, mining companies and those who farm large plantations. These companies assume charge of the convicts, work them as cheap labor and pay the states a handsome revenue for their labor. Nine-tenths of these convicts are Negroes. There are two reasons for this.

(1) The religious, moral and philanthropic forces of the country—all the agencies which tend to uplift and reclaim the degraded and ignorant, are in the hands of the Anglo-Saxon. Not only has very little effort been made by these forces to reclaim the Negro from the ignorance, immorality and shiftlessness with which he is charged, but he has always been and is now rigidly excluded from the enjoyment of those elevating influences toward which he felt voluntarily drawn. In communities where Negro population is largest and these counteracting influences most needed, the doors of churches, schools, concert halls, lecture rooms, Young Men's Christian Associations, and Women's Christian Temperance Unions, have always been and are now

closed to the Negro who enters on his own responsibility. Only as a servant or inferior being placed in one corner is he admitted. The white Christian and moral influences have not only done little to prevent the Negro becoming a criminal, but they have deliberately shut him out of everything which tends to make for good citizenship.

To have Negro blood in the veins makes one unworthy of consideration, a social outcast, a leper, even in the church. Two Negro Baptist Ministers, Rev. John Frank, the pastor of the largest colored church in Louisville, Ky., and Rev. C. H. Parish, President of Extein Norton University at Cane Spring, Ky., were in the city of Nashville, Tennessee, in May when the Southern Baptist Convention was in session. They visited the meeting and took seats in the body of the church. At the request of the Association, a policeman was called and escorted these men out because they would not take the seats set apart for colored persons in the back part of the Tabernacle. Both these men are scholarly, of good moral character, and members of the Baptist denomination. But they were Negroes, and that eclipsed everything else. This spirit is even more rampant in the more remote, densely populated plantation districts. The Negro is shut out and ignored, left to grow up in ignorance and vice. Only in the gambling dens and saloons does he meet any sort of welcome. What wonder that he falls into crime?

(2) The second reason our race furnishes so large a share of the convicts is that the judges, juries and other officials of the courts are white men who share these prejudices. They also make the laws. It is wholly in their power to extend clemency to white criminals and mete severe punishment to black criminals for the same or lesser crimes. The Negro criminals are mostly ignorant, poor and friendless. Possessing neither money to employ lawyers nor influential friends, they are sentenced in large numbers to long terms of imprisonment for petty crimes. The *People's Advocate*, a Negro journal, of Atlanta, Georgia, has the following observation on the prison showing of that state for 1892. "It is an astounding fact that 90 per cent of the state's convicts are colored; 194 white males and 2 white females; 1,710 colored males and 44 colored females. Is it possible that Georgia is so color prejudiced that she won't convict her white law-breakers. Yes, it is just so, but we hope for a better day."

George W. Cable, author of *The Grandissimes, Dr. Sevier,* etc., in a paper on "The Convict Lease System," read before a Prison Congress in Kentucky says: "In the Georgia penetentiary in 1880, in a total of nearly 1200 convicts, only 22 prisoners were serving as low a term as one year, only 52 others as low as two years, only 76 others as low a term as three years; while those who were under sentences of ten years and *over* numbered 538, although ten years, as the rolls show, is the *utmost* length of time that a convict can be expected to remain alive in a Georgia penetentiary. Six men were under sentence for simple assault and battery—mere fisticuffing—one of two years, two of five years, one of six years, one of seven and one of eight. For larceny, three men were serving under sentence of twenty years, five were sentenced each for fifteen years; one for fourteen years, six for twelve years; thirty-five for ten years, and 172 from one year up to nine years. In other words, a large majority of these 1200 convicts had for simple stealing, without breaking in or violence, been virtually condemned to be worked and misused to death. One man was under a twenty years' sentence for hog-stealing. Twelve men were sentenced to the South Carolina penetentiary on no other finding but a misdemeanor commonly atoned for by a fine of a few dollars, and which thousands of the state's inhabitants (white) are constantly committing with impunity—the carrying of concealed weapons. Fifteen others were sentenced for mere assault and battery. In Louisiana a man was sentenced to the penetentiary for 12 months for stealing five dollars worth of gunnysacks! Out of 2378 convicts in the Texas prison in 1882, only two were under sentence of less than two years length, and 509 of these were under twenty years of age. Mississippi's penetentiary roll for the same year showed 70 convicts between the ages of 12 and 18 years of age serving long terms. Tennessee showed 12 boys under 18 years of age, under sentences of more than a year; and the North Carolina penetentiary had 234 convicts under 20 years of age serving long terms."

Mr. Cable goes on to say in another part of his admirable paper: "In the Georgia convict force only 15 were whites among 215 who were under sentences of more than ten years." What is true of Georgia is true of the convict lease system everywhere. The details of vice, cruelty and death thus fostered by the states whose treasuries are enriched thereby, equals anything from Siberia. Men, women and children are herded together like cattle in the filthiest quarters and chained together while at work. The Chicago *Inter-Ocean* recently printed an interview with a young colored woman who was sentenced six months to the convict farm in Mississippi for fighting. The costs, etc., lengthened the time to 18 months. During her imprisonment she gave birth to two children, but lost the first one from premature confinement, caused by being tied up by the thumbs and punished for failure to do a full day's work. She and other women testified that they were forced to criminal intimacy with the guards and cook to get food to eat.

Correspondence to the Washington D.C. *Evening Star* dated Sept. 27, 1892, on this same subject has the following:

> The fact that the system puts a large number of criminals afloat in the community from the numerous escapes is not its worst feature. The same report shows that the mortality is fearful in the camps. In one camp it is stated that the mortality is 10 per cent per month, and in another even more than that. In these camps men and women are found chained together, and from twenty to twenty-five children have been born in captivity in the convicts' camps.
>
> Some further facts are cited with reference to the system in use in Tennessee. The testimony of a guard at the Coal Creek prison in Tennessee shows that prisoners, black and dirty from their work in the mines, were put into their rooms in the stockades without an opportunity to change their clothing or sufficient opportunity for cleanliness. Convicts were whipped, a man standing at the head and another at the feet, while a third applied the lash with both hands. Men who failed to perform their task of mining from two to four tons of coal per day were fastened to planks by the feet, then bent over a barrel and fastened by the hands on the other side, stripped and beaten with a strap. Out of the fifty convicts worked in the mines from one to eight were whipped per day in this manner. There was scarcely a day, according to the testimony of the witness, James Frazier, in which one or more were not flogged in this manner for failure to perform their day's task. The work in the mines was difficult and the air sometimes so bad that the men fell insensible and had to be hauled out. Their beds he described as "dirty, black and nasty looking." One of the convicts, testifying as to the kind of food given

them, said that the pea soup was made from peas containing weevils and added: "I have got a spoonful of weevils off a cup of soup." In many cases convicts were forced to work in water six inches deep for weeks at a time getting out coal with one-fourth of the air necessary for a healthy man to live in, forced to drink water from stagnant pools when mountain springs were just outside of the stockades,and the reports of the prison officials showing large numbers killed in attempting to escape.

The defense of this prison is based wholly upon its economy to the state. It is argued that it would cost large sums of money to build penitentiaries in which to confine and work the prisoners as is done in the Northern States, while the lease system brings the state a revenue and relieves it of the cost of building and maintaining prisons. The fact that the convicts labor is in this way brought into direct competition with free labor does not seem to be taken into account. The contractors, who get these laborers for 30 or 40 cents per day, can drive out of the market the man who employs free labor at $1 a day.

This condition of affairs briefly alluded to in detail in Tennessee and Georgia exists in other Southern States. In North Carolina the same system exists, except that only able-bodied convicts are farmed out. The death rates among the convicts is reported as greater than the death rate of New Orleans in the greatest yellow fever epidemic ever known. In Alabama a new warden with his natural instincts unblunted by familiarity with the situation wrote of it: "The system is a better training school for criminals than any of the dens of iniquity in our large cities. The system is a disgrace to the state and the reproach of the civilization and Christian sentiment of the age."

Every Negro so sentenced not only means able-bodied men to swell the state's number of slaves, but every Negro so convicted is thereby *disfranchised.*

It has been shown that numbers of Negro youths are sentenced to these penetentiaries every year and there mingle with the hardened criminals of all ages and both sexes. The execution of law does not cease with the incarceration of those of tender years for petty crimes. In the state of South Carolina last year Mildred Brown, a little thirteen year old colored girl was found guilty of murder in the first degree on the charge of poisoning a little white infant that she nursed. She was sentenced to be hanged. The Governor refused to commute her sentence, and on October 7th, 1892, at Columbia, South Carolina, she was hanged on the gallows. This made the second colored female hanged in that state within one month. Although tried, and in rare cases convicted for murder and other crimes, no white girl in this country ever met the same fate. The state of Alabama in the same year hanged a ten year old Negro boy. He was charged with the murder of a peddler.

CHAPTER IV

LYNCH LAW

By Ida B. Wells

"Lynch Law," says the *Virginia Lancet,* "as known by that appellation, had its origin in 1780 in a combination of citizens of Pittsylvania County, Virginia, entered into for the purpose of suppressing a trained band of horsethieves and counterfeiters whose well concocted schemes had bidden defiance to the ordinary laws of the land, and whose success encouraged and emboldened them in their outrages upon the community. Col. Wm. Lynch drafted the constitution for this combination of citizens, and hence "Lynch Law" has ever since been the name given to the summary infliction of punishment by private and unauthorized citizens."

This law continues in force to-day in some of the oldest states of the Union, where courts of justice have long been established, whose laws are executed by white Americans. It flourishes most largely in the states which foster the convict lease system, and is brought to bear mainly, against the Negro. The first fifteen years of his freedom he was murdered by masked mobs for trying to vote. Public opinion having made lynching for that cause unpopular, a new reason is given to justify the murders of the past 15 years. The Negro was first charged with attempting to rule white people, and hundreds were murdered on that pretended supposition. He is now charged with assaulting or attempting to assault white women. This charge, as false as it is foul, robs us of the sympathy of the world and is blasting the race's good name.

The men who make these charges encourage or lead the mobs which do the lynching. They belong to the race which holds Negro life cheap, which owns the telegraph wires, newspapers, and all other communication with the outside world. They write the reports which justify lynching by painting the Negro as black as possible, and those reports are accepted by the press associations and the world without question or investigation. The mob spirit has increased with alarming frequency and violence. Over a thousand black men, women and children have been thus sacrificed the past ten years. Masks have long since been thrown aside and the lynchings of the present day take place in broad daylight. The sheriffs, police and state officials stand by and see the work well done. The coroner's jury is often formed among those who took part in the lynching and a verdict, "Death at the hands of parties unknown to the jury" is rendered. As the number of lynchings have increased, so has the cruelty and barbarism of the lynchers. Three human beings were burned alive in civilized America during the first six months of this year (1893). Over one hundred have been lynched in this half year. They were hanged, then cut, shot and burned.

The following table published by the Chicago *Tribune* January, 1892, is submitted for thoughtful consideration.

1882,   52 Negroes murdered by mobs
1883,   39   "   "   "   "
1884,   53   "   "   "   "
1885,   77   "   "   "   "
1886,   73   "   "   "   "
1887,   70   "   "   "   "
1888,   72   "   "   "   "
1889,   95   "   "   "   "
1890, 100   "   "   "   "
1891, 169   "   "   "   "

Of this number

269 were charged with rape.
253   "   "   "   murder.
 44   "   "   "   robbery.
 37   "   "   "   incendiarism.
  4   "   "   "   burglary.

27	"	"	"	race prejudice.
13	"	"	"	quarreling with white men.
10	"	"	"	making threats.
7	"	"	"	rioting.
5	"	"	"	miscegenation.
32	"	"	"	no reasons given.

This table shows (1) that only one-third of nearly a thousand murdered black persons have been even charged with the crime of outrage. This crime is only so punished when white women accuse black men, which accusation is never proven. The same crime committed by Negroes against Negroes, or by white men against black women is ignored even in the law courts.

(2) That nearly as many were lynched for murder as for the above crime, which the world believes is the cause of all the lynchings. The world affects to believe that *white* womanhood and childhood, surrounded by their lawful protectors, are not safe in the neighborhood of the black man, who protected and cared for them during the four years of civil war. The husbands, fathers and brothers of those white women were away for four years, fighting to keep the Negro in slavery, yet not one case of assault has ever been reported!

(3) That "robbery, incendiarism, race prejudice, quarreling with white men, making threats, rioting, miscegenation (marrying a white person), and burglary," are capital offences punishable by death when committed by a black against a white person. Nearly as many blacks were lynched for these charges (and unproven) as for the crime of rape.

(4) That for nearly fifty of these lynchings no reason is given. There is no demand for reasons, or need of concealment for what no one is held responsible. The simple word of any white person against a Negro is sufficient to get a crowd of white men to lynch a Negro. Investigation as to the guilt or innocence of the accused is never made. Under these conditions, white men have only to blacken their faces, commit crimes against the peace of the community, accuse some Negro, or rest till he is killed by a mob. Will Lewis, an 18 year old Negro youth was lynched at Tullahoma, Tennessee, August 1891, for being "drunk and saucy to white folks."

The women of the race have not escaped the fury of the mob. In

Jackson, Tennessee, in the summer of 1886, a white woman died of poisoning. Her black cook was suspected, and as a box of rat poison was found in her room, she was hurried away to jail. When the mob had worked itself to the lynching pitch, she was dragged out of jail, every stitch of clothing torn from her body, and she was hung in the public court-house square in sight of everybody. Jackson is one of the oldest towns in the State, and the State Supreme Court holds its sittings there; but no one was arrested for the deed—not even a protest was uttered. The husband of the poisoned woman has since died a raving maniac, and his ravings showed that he, and not the poor black cook, was the poisoner of his wife. A fifteen year old Negro girl was hanged in Rayville, Louisiana, in the spring of 1892, on the same charge of poisoning white persons. There was no more proof or investigation of this case than the one in Jackson. A Negro woman, Lou Stevens, was hanged from a railway bridge in Hollendale, Mississippi, in 1892. She was charged with being accessory to the murder of her white paramour, who had shamefully abused her.

In 1892 there were 241 persons lynched. The entire number is divided among the following states.

Alabama	22	Montana	4
Arkansas	25	New York	1
California	3	North Carolina	5
Florida	11	North Dakota	1
Georgia	17	Ohio	3
Idaho	8	South Carolina	5
Illinois	1	Tennessee	28
Kansas	3	Texas	15
Kentucky	9	Virginia	7
Louisiana	29	West Virginia	5
Maryland	1	Wyoming	9
Mississippi	16	Arizona Ter.	3
Missouri	6	Oklahoma	2

Of this number 160 were of Negro descent. Four of them were lynched in New York, Ohio and Kansas; the remainder were murdered in the south. Five of this number were females. The charges for which they were lynched cover a wide range. They are as follows:

Rape	46	Attempted Rape	11
Murder	58	Suspected Robbery	4
Rioting	3	Larceny	1
Race prejudice	6	Self-defense	1
No cause given	4	Insulting women	2
Incendiarism	6	Desperadoes	6
Robbery	6	Fraud	1
Assault and Battery	1	Attempted murder	2

No offense stated, boy and girl 2

In the case of the boy and girl above referred to, their father, named Hastings, was accused of the murder of a white man; his fourteen year old daughter and sixteen year old son were hanged and their bodies filled with bullets. Then the father was also lynched. This was in November, 1892, at Jonesville, Louisiana.

A lynching equally as cold-blooded took place in Memphis, Tennessee, March, 1892. Three young colored men in an altercation at their place of business, fired on white men in self-defense. They were imprisoned for three days, then taken out by the mob and horribly shot to death. Thomas Moss, Will Stewart and Calvin McDowell, were energetic business men who had built up a flourishing grocery business. This business had prospered and that of a rival white grocer named Barrett had declined. Barrett led the attack on their grocery which resulted in the wounding of three white men. For this cause were three innocent men barbarously lynched, and their families left without protectors. Memphis is one of the leading cities of Tennessee, a town of seventy-five thousand inhabitants! No effort whatever was made to punish the murderers of these three men. It counted for nothing that the victims of this outrage were three of the best known young men of a population of thirty thousand colored people of Memphis. They were the officers of the company which conducted the grocery. Moss being the President, Stewart the Secretary of the Company and McDowell the Manager. Moss was in the Civil Service of the United States as letter carrier, and all three were men of splendid reputation for honesty, integrity and sobriety. But their murderers, though well known, have never been indicted, were not even troubled with a preliminary examination.

With law held in such contempt, it is not a matter of surprise that the same city—one of the so-called queen cities of the South—should again give itself over to a display of almost indescribable barbarism. This time the mob made no attempt to conceal its identity, but reveled in the contemplation of its feast of crime. Lee Walker, a colored man was the victim. Two white women complained that while driving to town, a colored man jumped from a place of concealment and dragged one of the two women from the wagon, but their screams frightened him away. Alarm was given that a Negro had made an attempted assault upon the women and bands of men set out to run him down. They shot a colored man who refused to stop when called. It was fully ten days before Walker was caught. He admitted that he did attack the women, but that he made no attempt to assault them; that he offered them no indecency whatever, of which as a matter of fact, they never accused him. He said he was hungry and he was determined to have something to eat, but after throwing one of the women out of the wagon, became frightened and ran away. He was duly arrested and taken to the Memphis jail. The fact that he was in prison and could be promptly tried and punished did not prevent the good citizens of Memphis from taking the law in their own hands, and Walker was lynched.

The *Memphis Commercial* of Sunday, July 23, contains a full account of the tragedy from which the following extracts are made.

> At 12 o'clock last night, Lee Walker, who attempted to outrage Miss Mollie McCadden, last Tuesday morning, was taken from the county jail and hanged to a telegraph pole just north of the prison. All day rumors were afloat that with nightfall an attack would be made upon the jail, and as everyone anticipated that a vigorous resistance would be made, a conflict between the mob and the authorities was feared.
>
> At 10 o'clock Capt. O'Haver, Sergt. Horan and several patrol men were on hand, but they could do nothing with the crowd. An attack by the mob was made on the door in the south wall and it yielded. Sheriff McLendon and several of his men threw themselves into the breach, but two or three of the storming party shoved by. They were seized by the police but were not subdued, the officers refraining from using their clubs. The entire mob might at first have been dispersed by ten policemen who would use their clubs, but the sheriff insisted that no violence be done.

The mob got an iron rail and used it as a battering ram against the lobby doors. Sheriff McLendon tried to stop them, and some one of the mob knocked him down with a chair. Still he counseled moderation and would not order his deputies and the police to disperse the crowd by force. The pacific policy of the sheriff impressed the mob with the idea that the officers were afraid, or at least would do them no harm, and they redoubled their efforts, urged on by a big switchman. At 12 o'clock the door of the prison was broken in with a rail.

As soon as the rapist was brought out of the door, calls were heard for a rope; then some one shouted "Burn him!" But there was no time to make a fire. When Walker got into the lobby a dozen of the men began beating and stabbing him. He was half dragged, half carried to the corner of Front street and the alley between Sycamore and Mill, and hung to a telephone pole.

Walker made a desperate resistance. Two men entered his cell first and ordered him to come forth. He refused and they failing to drag him out, others entered. He scratched and bit his assailants, wounding several of them severely with his teeth. The mob retaliated by striking and cutting him with fists and knives. When he reached the steps leading down to the door he made another stand and was stabbed again and again. By the time he reached the lobby his power to resist was gone, and he was shoved along through the mob of yelling, cursing men and boys, who beat, spat upon and slashed the wretch-like demon. One of the leaders of the mob fell, and the crowd walked ruthlessly over him. He was badly hurt—a jawbone fractured and internal injuries inflicted. After the lynching friends took charge of him.

The mob proceeded north on Front street with the victim, stopping at Sycamore street to get a rope from a grocery. "Take him to the iron bridge on Main street," yelled several men. The men who had hold of the Negro were in a hurry to finish the job, however, and when they reached the telephone pole at the corner of Front street and the first alley north of Sycamore they stopped. A hastily improvised noose was slipped over the Negro's head and several young men mounted a pile of lumber near the pole and threw the rope over one of the iron stepping pins. The Negro was lifted up until his feet were three feet above the ground, the rope was made taut, and a corpse dangled in midair. A big fellow who helped lead the mob pulled the Negro's legs until his neck cracked. The wretch's clothes had been torn off, and, as he swung, the man who pulled his legs mutilated the corpse.

One or two knife cuts, more or less, made little difference in the appearance of the dead rapist, however, for before the rope was around his neck his skin was cut almost to ribbons. One pistol shot was fired while the corpse was hanging. A dozen voices protested against the use of firearms, and there was no more shooting. The body was permitted to hang for half an hour, then it was cut down and the rope divided among those who lingered around the scene of the tragedy. Then it was suggested that the corpse be burned, and it was done. The entire performance, from the assault on the jail to the burning of the dead Negro was witnessed by a score or so of policemen and as many deputy sheriffs, but not a hand was lifted to stop the proceedings after the jail door yielded.

As the body hung to the telegraph pole, blood streaming down from the knife wounds in his neck, his hips and lower part of his legs also slashed with knives, the crowd hurled expletives at him, swung the body so that it was dashed against the pole, and, so far from the ghastly sight proving trying to the nerves, the crowd looked on with complaisance, if not with real pleasure. The Negro died hard. The neck was not broken, as the body was drawn up without being given a fall, and death came by strangulation. For fully ten minutes after he was strung up the chest heaved occasionally and there were convulsive movements of the limbs. Finally he was pronounced dead, and a few minutes later Detective Richardson climbed on a pile of staves and cut the rope. The body fell in a ghastly heap, and the crowd laughed at the sound and crowded around the prostrate body, a few kicking the inanimate carcass.

Detective Richardson, who is also a deputy coroner, then proceeded to impanel the following jury of inquest: J. S. Moody, A. C. Waldran, B. J. Childs, J. N. House, Nelson Bills, T. L. Smith, and A. Newhouse. After viewing the body the inquest was adjourned without any testimony being taken until 9 o'clock this morning. The jury will meet at the coroner's office, 51 Beale street, upstairs, and decide on a verdict. If no witnesses are forthcoming, the jury will be able to arrive at a verdict just the same, as all members of it saw the lynching. Then some one raised the cry of, "Burn him!" It was quickly taken up and soon resounded from a hundred throats. Detective Richardson for a long time, single handed, stood the crowd off. He talked and begged the men not to bring disgrace on the city by burning the body, arguing that all the vengeance possible had been wrought.

While this was going on a small crowd was busy starting a fire in the middle of the street. The material was handy. Some bundles of staves were taken from the adjoining lumber yard for kindling. Heavier wood was obtained from the same source, and coal oil from a neighboring grocery. Then the cries of "Burn him! Burn him!" were redoubled.

Half a dozen men seized the naked body. The crowd cheered. They marched to the fire, and giving the body a swing, it was landed in the middle of the fire. There was a cry for more wood, as the fire had begun to die owing to the long delay. Willing hands procured the wood, and it was piled up on the Negro, almost, for a time, obscuring him from view. The head was in plain view, as also were the limbs, and one arm which stood out high above the body, the elbow crooked, held in that position by a stick of wood. In a few moments the hands began to swell, then came great blisters over all the exposed parts of the body; then in places the flesh was burned away and the bones began to show through. It was a horrible sight, one which perhaps none there had ever witnessed before. It proved too much for a large part of the crowd and the majority of the mob left very shortly after the burning began.

But a large number stayed, and were not a bit set back by the sight of a human body being burned to ashes. Two or three white women, accompanied by their escorts, pushed to the front to obtain an unobstructed view and looked on with astonishing coolness and nonchalance. One man and woman brought a little girl, not over 12 years old, apparently their daughter, to view a scene which was calculated to drive sleep from the child's eyes for many nights, if not to produce a permanent injury to her nervous system. The comments of the crowd were varied. Some remarked on the efficacy of this style of cure for rapists, others rejoiced that men's wives and daughters were now safe from this wretch. Some laughed as the flesh cracked and blistered, and while a large number pronounced the burning of a dead body as an useless episode, not in all that throng was a word of sympathy heard for the wretch himself.

The rope that was used to hang the Negro, and also that which was used to lead him from the jail, were eagerly sought by relic hunters. They almost fought for a chance to cut off a piece of rope, and in an incredibly short time both ropes had disappeared and were scattered in the pockets of the crowd in sections of from an inch to six inches long. Others of the relic hunters remained until the ashes cooled to obtain such ghastly relics as the teeth, nails, and bits of charred skin of the immolated victim of his own lust. After burning the body the mob tied a rope around the charred trunk and dragged it down Main street to the court house, where it was hanged to a center pole. The rope broke and the corpse dropped with a thud, but it was again hoisted, the charred legs barely touching the ground. The teeth were knocked out and the finger nails cut off as souvenirs. The crowd made so much noise that the police interfered. Undertaker Walsh was telephoned for, who took charge of the body and carried it to his establishment, where it will be prepared for burial in the potter's field today.

A prelude to this exhibition of 19th century barbarism was the following telegram received by the Chicago *Inter-Ocean* at 2 o'clock, Saturday afternoon—ten hours before the lynching:

"Memphis, Tenn, July 22, To *Inter-Ocean*, Chicago.

Lee Walker, colored man, accused of raping white women, in jail here, will be taken out and burned by whites to-night. Can you send Miss Ida Wells to write it up? Answer. R. M. Martin, with *Public Ledger*."

The *Public Ledger* is one of the oldest evening daily papers in Memphis, and this telegram shows that the intentions of the mob were well-known long before they were executed. The personnel of the mob is given by the Memphis *Appeal-Avalanche*. It says, "At first it seemed as if a crowd of roughs were the principals, but as it increased in size, men in all walks of life figured as leaders, although the majority were young men."

This was the punishment meted out to a Negro, charged, not with rape, but attempted assault, and without any proof as to his guilt, for the women were not given a chance to identify him. It was only a little less horrible than the burning alive of Henry Smith, at Paris, Texas, February 1st, 1893, or that of Edward Coy, in Texarkana, Texas, February 20, 1892. Both were charged with assault on white women, and both were tied to the stake and burned while yet alive, in the presence of ten thousand persons. In the case of Coy, the white woman in the case, applied the match, even while the victim protested his innocence.

The cut which is here given is the exact reproduction of the photograph taken at the scene of the lynching at Clanton, Alabama, August, 1891. The cause for which the man was hanged is given in the words of the mob which were written on the back of the photograph, and they are also given. This photograph was sent to Judge A. W. Tourgée, of Mayville, N. Y.

In some of these cases the mob affects to believe in the Negro's guilt. The world is told that the white woman in the case identifies him or the prisoner "confesses." But in the lynching which took place in Barnwell County, South Carolina, April 24, 1893, the mob's victim, John Peterson escaped and placed himself under Governor Tillman's protection; not only did he declare his innocence, but offered to prove an alibi, by white witnesses. Before his witnesses could be brought, the mob arrived at the Governor's mansion and demanded the prisoner. He was given up, and although the white woman in the case said he was *not* the man, he was hanged 24 hours after, and over a thousand bullets fired into his body, on the declaration that "a crime had been committed and some one had to hang for it."

The lynching of C. J. Miller, at Bardwell, Kentucky, July 7, 1893, was on the same principle. Two white girls were found murdered near their home on the morning of July 5th; their bodies were horribly mutilated. Although their father had been instrumental in the prosecution and conviction of one of his white neighbors for murder, that was not considered as a motive. A hue and cry was raised that some Negro had committed rape and murder, and a search was immediately begun for a Negro. A bloodhound was put on the trail which he followed to the river and into the boat of a fisherman named Gordon. This fisherman said he had rowed a white man, or a very fair mulatto across the river at six o'clock the evening before. The bloodhound was carried across the river, took up the trail on the Missouri side, and ran about two hundred yards to the cottage of a white farmer, and there lay down refusing to go further.

Meanwhile a strange Negro had been arrested in Sikestown, Missouri, and the authorities telegraphed that fact to Bardwell, Kentucky. The sheriff, without requisition, escorted the prisoner to the Kentucky side and turned him over to the authorities who accompanied the mob. The prisoner was a man with dark brown skin; he said his name was Miller and that he had never been in Kentucky. The fisherman who had said the man he rowed over was white, when told by the

"Scene of Lynching at Clanton, Alabama, Aug. 1891"

sheriff that he would be held responsible as knowing the guilty man, if he failed to identify the prisoner, said Miller was the man. The mob wished to burn him then, about ten o'clock in the morning, but Mr. Ray, the father of the girls, with great difficulty urged them to wait till three o'clock that afternoon. Confident of his innocence, Miller remained cool, while hundreds of drunken, heavily armed men raged about him. He said: "My name is C. J. Miller, I am from Springfield, Ill., my wife lives at 716 North Second Street. I am here among you

FAC-SIMILE OF BACK OF PHOTOGRAPH.

"Fac-simile of Back of Photograph"

to-day looked upon as one of the most brutal men before the people. I stand here surrounded by men who are excited; men who are not willing to let the law take its course, and as far as the law is concerned, I have committed no crime, and certainly no crime gross enough to deprive me of my life or liberty to walk upon the green earth. I had some rings which I bought in Bismarck of a Jew peddler. I paid him $4.50 for them. I left Springfield on the first day of July and came to Alton. From Alton I went to East St. Louis, from there to Jefferson

Barracks, thence to Desoto, thence to Bismarck; and to Piedmont, thence to Poplar Bluff, thence to Hoxie, to Jonesboro, and then on a local freight to Malden, from there to Sikeston. On the 5th day of July, the day I was supposed to have committed the offense, I was at Bismarck."

Failing in any way to connect Miller with the crime, the mob decided to give him the benefit of the doubt and *hang, instead of burn him,* as was first intended. At 3 o'clock, the hour set for the execution, the mob rushed into the jail, tore off Miller's clothing and tied his shirt around his loins. Some one said the rope was "a white man's death," and a log-chain nearly a hundred feet in length, weighing nearly a hundred pounds was placed about his neck. He was led through the street in that condition and hanged to a telegraph pole. After a photograph of him was taken as he hung, his fingers and toes cut off, and his body otherwise horribly mutilated, it was burned to ashes. This was done within twelve hours after Miller was taken prisoner. Since his death, his assertions regarding his movements have been proven true. But the mob refused the necessary time for investigation.

No more appropriate close for this chapter can be given than an editorial quotation from that most consistent and outspoken journal the *Inter-Ocean.* Commenting on the many barbarous lynchings of these two months (June and July) in its issue of August 5th, 1893, it says:

"So long as it is known that there is one charge against a man which calls for no investigation before taking his life there will be mean men seeking revenge ready to make that charge. Such a condition would soon destroy all law. It would not be tolerated for a day by white men. But the Negroes have been so patient under all their trials that men who no longer feel that they can safely shoot a Negro for attempting to exercise his right as a citizen at the polls are ready to trump up any other charge that will give them the excuse for their crime. It is a singular coincidence that as public sentiment has been hurled against political murders there has been a corresponding increase in lynchings on the charge of attacking white women. The lynchings are conducted in much the same way that they were by the Ku Klux Klans when Negroes were mobbed for attempting to vote. The one great difference is in the cause which the mob assigns for its action.

The real need is for a public sentiment in favor of enforcing the law and giving every man, white and black, a fair hearing before the lawful tribunals. If the plan suggested by the Charleston *News and Courier* will do this let it be done at once. No one wants to shield a fiend guilty of these brutal attacks upon unprotected women. But the Negro has as good a right to a fair trial as the white man, and the South will not be free from these horrible crimes of mob law so long as the better class of citizens try to find excuse for recognizing Judge Lynch."

CHAPTER V

THE PROGRESS OF THE AFRO-AMERICAN SINCE EMANCIPATION

By I. Garland Penn

That the Afro-American has made some progress in education, in the professions, in the accumulation of wealth and literature, and how much, this chapter will show. To determine the progress of the race in education it is necessary to know the relative progress in the increase of population since Emancipation, the number who could read and write, and the number who were in school. According to the census report there were in this country in

1850,	3,638,808	Afro-Americans.
1860,	4,441,830	"
1870,	4,880,009	"
1880,	6,580,793	"
1890,	7,470,040	"

The census of 1860 shows an increase of 703,022 in ten years; that of 1870 shows an increase of 438,179 in ten years; that of 1880 shows an increase of 1,700,784 in ten years; that of 1890 shows an increase of 889,247 in ten years. From 1850 to 1890 the race increased 3,831,232 persons.

It was hardly considered probable that any considerable number of the freedmen would at once seize the opportunity for immediate education as they did when the first ray of hope and light beamed upon them from the philanthropic north. Yet the Afro-American, as upon a moment's thought availed himself of the opportunities which were offered under the Freedmens' Bureau, the first organized effort to educate the freedmen. With this effort came in close succession efforts of the church and those of a general character, so that we now have the following schools for the training of Afro-American youth: The American Baptist Home Mission Society; the American Missionary Association; the Presbyterian Board of Missions for Freedmen; the Freedmen's Aid and Southern Educational Society; the Colored Evangelistic Fund (Southern Presbyterian Church); Negro Education and Evangelization Society (Christian Church); the Educational Society in the United Presbyterian Church; the Protestant Episcopal Commission; the African Methodist Episcopal Church; the African Methodist Episcopal Zion Church; the Colored Methodist Episcopal Church in America; the Colored Baptist Church. In the non-denominational schools of the United States the number of schools for the Higher, Secondary Normal, Graded and Common Schools' training is 379. Number of teachers 1,775, of which 646 are Afro-Americans. Number of students in 1892, 52,443.

The number of teachers in the Public School system of the United States reported by the United States Census in 1890 were 23,866, and the number of pupils seeking education under the free school system were 1,460,447. These figures reported in 1890 can safely be relied upon as an approximation for 1892, since year by year the Afro-American is becoming more awakened to a sense of duty in respect to the training of his offspring. Taking the census figures for '90 as a basis for '92, and adding the 646 Afro-American teachers in denominational and non-denominational schools, we have a sum total approximation of 24,510 Afro-American teachers in the United States with 1,512,890 pupils. The showing as to teachers is a bright ray of hope for the Afro-American's future when the fact is considered in all of its bearings that these 24,510, or in round numbers 25,000 (if the reader will allow 490 teachers graduated and obtaining employment during '90 and '92), have been prepared and put into the field during a quarter of a century, very little more than the school life allotted an individual.

As to pupils the showing is more remarkable. Five years after the surrender, in 1870, only a tenth of the Afro-American children eligible to school opportunities were actually reported therein. In 1890 we find that within a fraction, ONE-HALF of the eligibles are reported in school. Figures can be given to authenticate this statement upon application, as they are only omitted for sake of space which is precious.

In 1870 there were according to census figures 2,789,679 persons of color above the age of ten years who could not read nor write. If we should make an approximation of a million for persons of color under ten years (which we think every fair minded reader will accept as just) we should have 3,789,679 who could not read or write twenty years ago. With a population of 4,880,009 we should have one and a tenth million of people of African descent who could read and write in '70. It is unfair to say that the increase from '70 to '93 should be less than four times that of '70 under great and constantly increasing educational facilities in all the departments of state and church education.

If the reader accepts the statement that the great educational endeavors of twenty years in all departments and all lines justify an increase four times as large as that of '70 we shall have four and four-tenth millions of Afro-Americans who can now read and write. The writer maintains that of this balance of illiteracy, a majority are ex-slaves; elderly persons who may not read the letter but who are yet intelligent by contact and association. At least two hundred thousand boys and girls of the race to-day are private students. In a certain city there are ten private night schools in which an aggregate of 300 boys are training in the light of knowledge and education by night, wealth and habits of industry by day.

Bishop Atticus G. Haygood says, "The most unique and altogether wonderful chapter in the history of education is that which tells the story of the education of the Negroes of the south since 1865."

Rev. C. C. Smith, D. D., Cor. Secretary of the "Negro Education and Evangelization Society" of the Christian Church, carefully studies the problem and awakes to find himself making this admission that "the Negroes desire for education considering his past environments is 'The Eighth Wonder.'"

THE PROFESSIONS

The black man's desire for professional training has been a subject for adverse criticism. It has been alleged that he is acquiring too much professional training for the support which conditions among the race offer him. The professions in which he is most largely represented, are the ministry and teaching. These claim our largest numbers for many reasons, prominent among them is the patent fact that a people who would rise must have religious and secular training. An admission that these professions for the first few years after the Civil War were besieged because of the ease by which employment could be obtained in them is perhaps just, but for the past ten years these charges are met with the declarations of Conferences, Conventions, Associations, Presbyteries, Synods, Superintendents, School Boards, etc., that none need apply except the well equipped. Of the 23,866 common school teachers in the Union, two-thirds are Normal and High School Graduates. The Theological institutions have graduated over 500 preachers and five times as many left school in their second and third years, who are now in the ministry doing yeoman service.

These professions have been again most largely followed for the reason that the facilities were greater, help larger and such training more easily obtained. Since and prior to the organization of schools for training of Afro-American physicians 417 graduates in the practice of Medicine have come forth occupying to-day honorable station in the medical jurisprudence of our common country. There are not twenty-five Afro-American physicians who are failures either as to their knowledge of medicine or financial condition. Their practice takes the wide range of from $1,000 to $5,000 per annum. Their residences are generally the finest and most representative in the towns in which they are located, and they rapidly accumulate wealth because they are skillful and successful in their profession. The Medical Afro-Americans are yearly organizing state associations and bringing their interests closer together. A graduate of Meharry Medical School, now practicing physician at Jackson, Tennessee, publishes a Medical Magazine, known as the Medical and Surgical Observer. While a staff of colored physicians and trained nurses manages one of the best hospitals in Chicago—the Provident Hospital. In dentistry there are 33 practicing physicians in the south, and nearly the same number in the north. In Pharmacy over 75 have been graduated. The profession in which Afro-Americans have met the sharpest opposition and the strongest competition has been the law. There have been graduated from the Law Schools together with those who have taken private courses, about 300, among whom we find men of eminent legal ability, one a Circuit Court Commissioner, several Judges, numbers of Clerks of Courts, several District Commonwealth and City Attorneys. They are also Deans and Professors of Law in their legal schools, the students of which have not been turned down by any Court or Board in examination. Greater credit, perhaps, is due these advocates for a successful stand maintained, than is due those of any other profession. Besides sharp competition with white lawyers, open and free before a white jury in a land pregnant with prejudice, the Afro-American lawyer has had also to contend with his black fellow citizens whose lack of confidence in the black lawyer is evident for the reason that prejudice, fear and oppression have been elements sufficient in themselves to arouse and determine a pre-judgment.

An eminent newspaper of the south makes the statement that 250 black lawyers in the Union have practice ranging from $1,000 to $20,000 per annum. The writer knows a black lawyer in his own city who handles $150,000 annually. As in medicine so in law. State Bar Associations are being formed in almost every state of the south for legal advice, union and strength.

In Literature

Our history shows that prior to 1861, there had been thirty-five works of Afro-American authorship published and sold. In the earlier days of 1792, America's first poet was Phillis Wheatley, a little black girl, who was brought to this country in a slave ship. After careful education by her white friends, she published a book of poems. The purity of style, simplicity of expression, and refinement of feeling shown in these poems, caused many to doubt their authorship. This doubt was set at rest by her master John Wheatley of Boston, and the leading ministers of the city. They wrote a letter in which they declared Phillis to be the author of the poems published by her. Near the same time Benjamin Banneker, a Negro of Virginia, made his own measurements and calculations, and published an almanac. Since 1865 over 100 books have been published by Afro-American writers. They have been mainly histories of the race, autobiographies, poems, and works on science, fiction, religion and general literature. A Greek Grammar for beginners, by W. S. Scarborough, of Wilberforce Ohio, is in use in the schools of Ohio.

In Journalism

The first journal published in race interest was Freedom's Journal, issued in 1827, in New York City. At the present time there are 206 journals and four magazines published by the colored people of the country. At a recent meeting of the State Press Association of Virginia, the statement was made that the Afro-American newspapers of that state owned property amounting to $25,000. At least two-thirds of these publications are made in their own offices and on their own presses. Several of our journalists hold responsible positions on the leading dailies as editors of departments and reporters. Essays, short stories and poems by race writers have appeared in the North American Review, Arena, Harper's, Forum, Atlantic Monthly, Frank Leslie, Our Day, The Independent, The Sunday School Journal of the Methodist Church, and other magazines of the country.

In Church

Bishop Haygood, of M. E. Church South, very truthfully writes in one of his books that all of the Negro's interest, particularly his social life, centers in his church. The denominations in which the Afro-American is most largely found are: Methodist Episcopal, African Methodist Episcopal, African Methodist Episcopal Zion, Colored

Methodist Episcopal Church in America, the Methodist Protestant, the African Union Methodist Protestant, the Union American Methodist Episcopal Church, the Zion Union Apostolic Church, the Evangelist Missionary Church in America, Congregational Methodist Church, Christian Church, Protestant Episcopal, Cumberland Presbyterian, Presbyterian Church in America, Presbyterian Church in the United States, United Presbyterian Church, Lutherans, Congregationalist and Regular Baptist Churches.

The numbers in these denominations are some very large and some small. The division and separation, particularly in the Methodist Churches, are upon very slight and inconsequential grounds. Of these denominations there are about 21,801 organizations, 22,153 church edifices with a seating capacity of perhaps 6 millions (since an estimate cannot be made in some cases on account of the absence of separate statistics on this last item). The African Methodist Episcopal, African Methodist Episcopal Zion, the Colored Methodist Episcopal Church in America, the African Union Methodist Protestant Church, the Union American Methodist Episcopal Church, The Zion Union Apostolic, the Evangelist Missionary Church in America, the Congregational Methodist Church, the Cumberland Presbyterian Church and regular Colored Baptist Church own 920 halls with a seating capacity of 78,289. The value of the Afro-Americans' church property may be approximated at $22,570,882; the number of church members, 2,613,154. This estimate exceeds that of Dr. H. K. Carroll, Special Agent for the U. S. Census Bureau on Churches, in the Sept. *Forum* by over two thousand members, for the reason that special care was taken in the separation of Afro-American membership from those of the whites, where no separate returns are given in the U. S. Census bulletins. The churches built by Afro-Americans are very fine. The Afro-American who makes five dollars per week, usually contributes a fifth of that to his church.

There are 26 bishops in the distinctively Afro-American Methodist bodies. The general officers are men of ability. Their colleges, normal schools and academies are manned by Afro-American presidents, principals, professors and instructors. Their members contributed for eight years ending in 1892, over $600,000 for the cause of education, in churches where the Anglo-Saxon and Afro-American are still blending their interests. Four Afro-Americans are at the head of four of the Methodist Episcopal schools, Professors hold responsible chairs, and writers are being recognized in the literary channels of the church. In the Presbyterian church a similar condition prevails. At the General Assembly, which met during April in Washington, an Afro-American President, Dr. D. J. Saunders, was heard in behalf of his school and its endowment, etc. He was there and then pledged $400,000 for the benefit of Biddle University, Charlotte, N. C. There are 57 Afro-American Presidents of Afro-American colleges, denominational and otherwise. For the scholastic year, 1891–2, of the $834,646.41 contributed or expended in Afro-American education by various societies, denominations, etc., $316,446.92 was contributed by the Afro-American himself, being nearly one-half of the entire expenditure. Many of the largest edifices and finest church buildings are those owned by Afro-American congregations. "In three large cities of the South (said a Southern

"Porter Hall—One of the main Buildings containing Office and Recitation Rooms, of Tuskegee Institute"

man in the writer's presence) the finest churches are 'Nigger' churches." One of the seven finest Sunday schools in the 27,493 of the great
Methodist Episcopal Church is an Afro-American School, the plan
of which has been adopted by several leading Anglo-Saxon Sunday
Schools.

HIS WEALTH AND BUSINESS INTERESTS

The wealth of the Afro-American has been fixed by statisticians at
the following figures:

Alabama	$9,200,125	North Carolina	$11,010,652
Oregon	85,000	Nevada	250,000
Connecticut	500,155	Arkansas	8,100,315
Delaware	1,200,179	California	4,006,209
North Dakota	76,459	Colorado	3,100,472
Florida	7,900,040	Dist. Columbia	5,300,633
Utah	75,000	South Dakota	175,225
Iowa	2,500,372	Georgia	10,415,330
Chicago alone	2,500,000	Illinois	8,300,511
Indiana	4,004,113	Indian Territory	600,000
Kentucky	5,900,000	Kansas	3,900,222
Maine	175,211	Louisiana	18,100,528
Missouri	6,600,340	Mississippi	13,400,213
Minnesota	1,100,236	Maryland	9,900,735
Montana	120,000	Michigan	4,800,000
New York	17,400,756	New Jersey	3,300,185
New Mexico	290,000	New Hampshire	300,125
Nebraska	2,500,000	Virginia	4,900,000
Massachusetts	9,004,122	Ohio	7,800,325
Rhode Island	3,400,000	Pennsylvania	15,300,648
South Carolina	12,500,000	Texas	18,010,545
Tennessee	10,400,211	Vermont	1,100,371
West Virginia	5,600,721	Washington	573,000
		Wyoming	231,115

The total amount of property owned by the race is $263,000,000.
This report, which is an under-estimate, has been going the rounds
and accepted as a most remarkable showing. It is an underestimate by

at least ten millions. For instance in the state of Virginia, according to the report of the Auditor of Public Accounts, the Afro-American property in the state was valued at $9,425,578. This is over four million and a half more than the above table. In Texas the property interests of the Afro-American are estimated at twenty millions, two millions more than the above table gives. The Comptroller of South Carolina informs the writer that the figures above given for South Carolina are very much below the real estimate. With these corrections and one or two exceptions, the figures are in the main correct. With these corrections, we should have an estimated wealth of not less than $275,000,000 for the Afro-American population of the United States. This added to Church property would give $300,000,000.

Until the recent failure of the Penny Savings Bank of Chattanooga, due to money loaned and inability to make collections, the Afro-American had five banking institutions. The remaining four are doing a splendid business. There are not less than thirty-five Building, Loan and Co-operative Associations on a firm footing and doing legitimate business subject to the regular state and municipal investigation. Lack of space prevents the details of the operations, assets and liabilities of each of these efforts.

This has been accumulated in spite of the failure of the Freedman's Savings Bank. This bank was established under the National Government in 1866, with branch offices in the different states. In this bank the colored people deposited in the five years succeeding the war, nearly fifty-seven million dollars. As the result of bad management it failed in 1871, and the savings from the Negro's scanty wages were thus largely swept away. The confidence thus shaken in the outset has never been entirely restored.

As Tradesmen and General Laborers

Until recent years the Afro-American has had a monopoly of the general and trade labor of the south. In recent times skilled labor has been the demand, and in many instances he has been driven out of the field, but in every southern city there are Afro-Americans who can do the best work in all trades. The writer knows of an instance not two weeks from date of this writing. A very large church is being remodeled and a handsome pressed brick front is a part of the improvement. There could not be found in a city of 22,000 inhabitants masons who could lay these brick satisfactorily. In response to a telegram four Afro-Americans were secured, and at this writing, August 2nd, 1893, the front is nearing completion. A more beautiful piece of work of its kind has not been done in the city. One of these men is a graduate of one of our best industrial schools.

The dearth in recent years of our mechanics is due to age, infirmities and death of those who were taught the trades in slavery; but the large and intelligent class of mechanics, who are being sent out from our mechanical schools, men whose head, heart and hands are trained, is remedying the deficiency. Nearly 6,000 of our young people were enrolled in the Industrial departments of Afro-American schools last year, and it is a fortunate thing that nearly all of the large schools of the south now have their industrial departments.

Rev. J.C. Hartzell, D. D., Secretary of the Freedman's Aid and Southern Education Society was heard once to say "A man said to me 'I will tell you one thing you cannot make a mechanic out of a Negro.' I took a wheel out of my pocket and showed it to him. I said 'there came into our shop at Central Tennessee College a black young man with no white blood in his veins, who had never seen such a machine before as that required to make this wheel. The manager had a lot of these wheels to make. This wheel must be made very exact; there must not be the least variation in any of its parts. The manager asked the young man if he could make wheels, and he said he would try; he did try and cut twenty-six hundred of these cogs before he made a variation.' I wonder if there is any other wheel of the kind ever made by a Negro. We are proud, first, that we have such places, and second, because such places are filled up with black boys." This was done in the school of Mechanic Arts, at Central Tennessee College, Nashville, Tennessee. From the same school the writer saw a ten inch telescope exhibited at the General Conference of the Methodist Episcopal church at Omaha, Neb., May, 1892. This telescope is now in the observatory at Laurence University, Appleton, Wisconsin, having been built for that purpose. Three of the Professors' homes at Clark University, Atlanta, Ga., were built by the industrial students.

The largest agricultural and industrial features are connected with the following schools: Hampton Normal and Agricultural Institute, Tuskegee Normal and Industrial Institute, Bishop College, Central Tennessee, Claflin University, Clark University, Shaw University, Spellman Female Institute, Straight University, Talladega College, Tougaloo University, State Normal and Industrial School (Alabama) and others. These with others are yearly sending forth skilled labor which demands a consideration and can easily compete in all lines of industry, where prejudice does not debar them. Tuskegee Institute, situated in the heart of the "black belt" in Alabama was founded by Booker T. Washington, an Afro-American. From a small one-room beginning twelve years ago, he has a school property there of 21 buildings and 1,400 acres of land, and this property is valued at $180,000.

Of this school, Mrs. A. J. Cooper, in "A Voice from the South," the ablest book yet written by a Negro, on the Negro, says: "In the heart of what is known as the 'Black Belt,' of Alabama and within easy reach of the great cotton plantations of Georgia, Mississippi and

"Phelps' Hall—Used as a Bible Training Department"

Florida, a devoted young colored man ten years ago started a school with about thirty Negro children assembled in a comical looking shanty at Tuskegee. His devotion was contagious and his work grew; an abandoned farm of 100 acres was secured and that gradually grew to 640 acres, largely woodland, on which a busy and prosperous school is located; and besides, a supply farm was added, of heavy rich land, 800 acres, from which grain and sugar cane are the main products. Since 1881 2,947 students have been taught here, of whom 102 have graduated, while 200 more have received training to fit them to do good work as teachers, intelligent farmers and mechanics. The latest enrollment shows girls 247; boys, 264. Of the 102 graduates, 70 per cent are teachers, ministers and farmers. They usually combine teaching and farming. Three are printers (learned the trades at school), one is a tinner, one a blacksmith, one a wheelwright, three are merchants, three are carpenters, others are in the professions or filling miscellaneous positions."

Another institution founded by the race, is the Provident Hospital, of Chicago. Prejudice because of color has denied our doctors opportunity for practical surgical work, and refused our young women who wish to become trained nurses, admittance to the hospital training schools of the country. Out of this necessity grew the Provident Hospital, which is owned and managed by colored men. It has been in operation a little over two years; patients of every color and all creeds are treated by Afro-American nurses and physicians, and the cures there effected have attracted more than local attention in the medical world. One of the most recent cases was by a knife wound in the pericardium which was sewed up after the removal of a section of the ribs. The patient has since recovered. The training school has graduated four nurses, and has many more applicants for training than can be accommodated.

As a general laborer, the Negro needs no introduction. He has built the railroads of the South, watered and nurtured its fields, reclaimed its swamps, beautified its cities, and caused the waste places to blossom as a rose. Besides general laborers and skilled artizans, the race has made some record in inventions. The following list is taken from the columns of *The Colored American,* July 8th, 1893, of Washington, D.C.

A partial list of patents granted by the United States for inventions by colored persons:

Improved Gridiron—Joseph Hawkins, West Windsor, N. J., March 26, 1845. No. 3,973.

Animal Trap—Henry Lee, Richmond, Va., Feb., 12, 1867. 61,941.

Shoe—W. A. Dietz, Albany, N. Y., April 30, 1867. 64,205.

Corn-stalk Harvester—Wm. Murray, Alexandria, Va., Feb. 1, 1870. 99,463.

Shield for Infantry and Artillerymen—Hardy Spears, Snow Hill, N. C., Dec. 27, 1870. 110,599.

Locomotive Smoke-stack—Landrow Bell, Washington, D. C., May 23, 1871. 115,153.

Fire Extinguisher—T. J. Martin, Dowagiac, Mich., March 26, 1872. 125,063.

Dough Kneader—Landrow Bell, Washington, D. C., Dec. 10, 1872. 133,823.

Cotton Cultivator—E. H. Sutton, Edenton, N. C., April 7, 1874. 149,543.

Joiners' Clamp—David A. Fisher, Jr., Washington, D. C., April 20, 1875. 162,281.

Process for Preparing Cocoanut for Domestic Use—Alex. P. Ashbourne, Oakland, Cal., June 1, 1875. 163,962.

Life-Preserving Stool—Henry H. Nash, Baltimore, Md., Oct. 5, 1875. 168,519.

Biscuit Cutter—Alex. P. Ashbourne, Oakland, Cal., Nov. 30, 1875. 170,460.

Furniture Castor—David A. Fisher, Jr., Washington, D. C., March 14, 1876. 174,794.

Range—T. A. Carrington, Baltimore, Md., July 25, 1876. 180,323.

Treating Cocoanut—Alex. P. Ashbourne, Oakland, Cal., Aug. 21, 1877. 184,287.

Rotary Engines—B. H. Taylor, Rosedale, Miss., April 23, 1878. 202,888.

Fire Escape Ladder—J. R. Winters, Chambersburg, Pa., May 7, 1878. 203,517.

Printing Press—W. A. Lavelette, Washington, D. C., Sept. 17, 1878. 208,184.

Library Table—W. R. Davis, Jr., New York City, Sept. 24, 1873. 208,378.

Fire Escape Ladder—Jos. R. Winters, Chambersburg, Pa., April 8, 1879. 214,224.

Ladder Scaffold Support—Wm. Bailis, Princeton, N. J., Aug. 5, 1879. 218,154.

Refining Cocoanut Oil—A. P. Ashbourne, Boston, Mass., July 17, 1880. 230,518.

File Holder—Traverse B. Pinn, Alexandria, Va., Aug. 17, 1880. 231,355.

Eye Protector—Powell Johnson, Barton, Ala., Nov. 2, 1880. 234,039.

Life Saving Apparatus—J. Wormley, Washington, D. C., May 24, 1881. 242,091.

Corn Planter Check Row—R. W. Alexander, Galesburg, Ill., April 18, 1882. 256,610.

Lasting Machine for Shoes—J. E. Matzeliger, Lynn, Mass., (Cuban), March 20, 1883. 274,207.

Ventilator for Railroad Cars—H. H. Reynolds, Detroit, Mich., April 3, 1883. 275,271.

Shutter and Fastening therefor—Jonas Cooper, Washington, D. C., May 1, 1883. 276,563.

Combined Truss and Bandage—Leonard D. Bailey, Washington, D. C., Sept. 25, 1883. 285,545.

Hand Corn-Shelling Device—Lockrum Blue, Washington, D. C., May 20, 1884. 298,937.

Steam Boiler Furnace—Granville T. Woods, Cincinnati, Ohio, June 3, 1884. 399,894.

Telephone Transmitter—Granville T. Woods, Cincinnati, Ohio, Dec. 2, 1884. 308,817.

Apparatus for Transmission of Messages by Electricity—Granville T. Woods, Cincinnati, Ohio, April 7, 1885; assigned to the American Bell Telephone Co., Boston, Mass. 315,368.

Horse Shoe—J. Ricks, Washington, D. C., March 30, 1886. 338,781.

Receptacle for Storing and Preserving Papers—Henry Brown, Washington, D. C., Nov.2, 1886. 352,036.

Gate Latch—Samuel Pugsley, New Rochelle, N. Y., Feb. 15, 1887. 357,787.

Motor—Joseph Gregory, Bogensville, S. C., April 26, 1887. 361,937.

Game Table—Wm. R. Davis, New York City, N. Y., May 10, 1887. 362,611.

Gong and Signal Chairs for Hotels—Miss Mariam E. Benjamin, Washington, D. C., July 17, 1888. 396,289.

Spring Horse Shoe—Moses Payne, Bellevue, Ky., Dec. 11, 1888. 394,398.

Instantaneous Detachment for Harnesses—J. S. Coolidge, Washington, D. C., Nov. 13, 1888. 392,908.

Folding Chair—Sadgwar & Purdy, Washington, D. C., June 11, 1889. 405,117.

Device for Preventing Back Flow of Water in Cellars—Hugh M. Browne, Washington, D. C., April 29, 1890. 426,429.

Electric Switch for Railroads—Philip B. Downing, Boston, Mass., July 17, 1890. 430,118.

Blind Stop—Abram Pugsley, Jamestown, R. I., July 29, 1890, 433,306.

Shutter Worker—Abram Pugsley, Jamestown, R. I., Aug. 5, 1890.

Water Evaporators for Hot Air Registers—Andrew F. Hilyer, Washington, D. C., Aug. 26, 1890. 435,095.

Safety Gate for Bridges—H. H. Reynolds, Detroit, Mich., Oct. 7, 1890. 437,937.

Drill for Boring and Reaming—J. R. Watts, Springfield, Ill., May 5, 1891. 451,789.

Lasting Machine—Sept. 22, 1891—Jean Earnest Matzeliger (dec'd), Lynn, Mass., (Cuban). 459,899.

Car Coupling—James Dixon, Cincinnati, Ohio, March, 29, 1892.

Bracket for Miners' Lamps—J. R. Watts, Springfield, Ill., March 7, 1893. 493,137.

Railroad Signal—A. B. Blackburn, Springfield, Ohio, Dec. 23, 1884. 309,517.

Railway Signal—A. B. Blackburn, Springfield, Ohio, Jan. 10, 1888. 376,362.

Spring Seat for Chairs—A. B. Blackburn, Springfield, Ohio, April 3, 1888. 380,420.

Cash Carrier—A. B. Blackburn, Springfield, Ohio, Oct. 23, 1888. 391,577.

Also fifteen (15) patents as follows to Elijah McCoy, of Detroit, Mich.,
    for his inventions in Steam Engine and Railway Lubricating Cups:
    Nos. 129,843; 139,407; 173,032; 179,585; 255,443; 261,166; 270,238;
        320,379; 357,491; 283,745; 383,746; 418,130; 465,875; 470,263; and 472,066.
Propeller for Vessels—Geo. Toliver, Philadelphia, Pa., April 28, 1891.
    451,086.
L. W. Benjamin, Boston, Mass., 497,747.

In the Realm of Art

With most meagre incentive, our race has many amateur artists
who possess great native talent, and several who have won recognition for their ability as professionals. E. N. Bannister, of Providence,

"Provident Hospital and Training School"

Rhode Island, had a picture in the Centennial Exposition of Philadelphia, in 1876, which was awarded one of the medals of the first class. This picture "Under the Oaks" was purchased for fifteen hundred dollars by a wealthy Boston gentleman. C. E. Porter of Hartford, Connecticut exhibits in the National Academy of Design of New York, in which city he has a studio. H. O. Tanner of Philadelphia, studied in his native city at the Academy of Fine Arts and has exhibited in the art galleries of New York, Chicago, Louisville, Cincinnati, Washington and Paris. He has spent the past two years abroad prosecuting his studies under Benjamin Constant and Jean Paul Laurens, in the Institute of France. On his return to this country they gave him a letter of recommendation. He belongs to the American Art Association in Paris and won the prize for a sketch of "The Deluge," from the Julian School of Art in 1892, and another for a sketch of "Peasant Life in Brittany." Mr. Tanner thinks the picturesque in our own race life can best be interpreted by one of ourselves and will exhibit this winter a picture representing one phase of Negro life. He has called it "The First Lesson." As a study it is regarded by art critics as the best thing he has done. Mr. Tanner is not yet thirty-five years of age.

We have a number of excellent crayon portrait painters who have made little effort to acquaint the world with their gifts. We also have a representative in

The Art of Sculpture

Miss Edmonia Lewis, a young, ignorant girl, saw the statue of Benjamin Franklin on a first visit to Boston and exclaimed, "I can make a stone man!" Wm. Lloyd Garrison introduced her to a leading Boston sculptor, who gave her some clay and the model of a human foot, which she copied. From this beginning, Miss Lewis has now a studio of her own in Rome. Here she has executed work which has brought her the patronage of noted men and women. Her best works are busts of Charles Sumner, and Abraham Lincoln, "Hiawatha's Wooing," "Forever Free," "Hagar in the Wilderness" and the "Madonna."

IN MUSIC

"Blind Tom" our musical prodigy imitates on the piano all sounds, and plays the most difficult classical music after hearing it once rendered. He has composed the "Battle of Manasses," in which the firing of cannon, marching of troops and playing of the bands are perfectly reproduced. Madame Selika, "The Black Patti" (Madame Jones), and Mrs. Nellie Brown Mitchell are the best of numbers of splendid vocalists who are training every year in the art the race loves best. Gussie L. Davis is one of the most popular song writers of the day. The Fisk Jubilee Singers have made the music of the American Negro known throughout the world. So eminent an authority as Dr. Antonin Dvorak, the great Bohemian composer, voluntarily says: "I am now satisfied that the future music of this country must be founded upon what are called the Negro melodies. This must be the real foundation of any serious and original school of composers to be developed in the United States. When I first came here last year I was impressed with this idea and it has developed into a settled conviction. These beautiful and varied themes are the product of the soil. They are American. I would like to trace out the individual authorship of the Negro melodies, for it would throw a great deal of light upon the question I am deeply interested in at present.

"These are the folk songs of America and your composers must turn to them. All of the great musicians have borrowed from the songs of the common people. Beethoven's most charming scherzo is based upon what might now be considered a skillfully handled Negro melody. I have myself gone to the simple, half forgotten tunes of the Bohemian peasants for hints in my most serious work. Only in this way can a musician express the true sentiment of his people. He gets into touch with the common humanity of his country.

"In the Negro melodies of America I discover all that is needed for a great and noble school of music. They are pathetic, tender, passionate, melancholy, solemn, religious, bold, merry, gay or what you will. It is music that sets itself to any mood or any purpose. There is nothing in the whole range of composition that cannot be supplied with themes from this source. The American musician understands these tunes, and they move sentiment in him. They appeal to his imagination because of their associations.

"When I was in England one of the ablest musical critics in London complained to me that there was no distinctively English school of music, nothing that appealed particularly to the British mind and heart. I replied to him that the composers of England had turned their backs upon the fine melodies of Ireland and Scotland instead of mak-

Hanging of C. J. Miller, at Bardwell, Kentucky, July 7th, 1893.

"Hanging of C. J. Miller, at Bardwell, Kentucky, July 7th, 1893"

ing them the essence of an English school. It is a great pity that English musicians have not profited out of this rich store. Somehow the old Irish and Scotch ballads have not seized upon or appealed to them. I hope it will not be so in this country, and I intend to do all in my power to call attention to these treasures of melody which you have.

"Among my pupils in the National Conservatory of Music I have discovered strong talents. There is one young man upon whom I am building strong expectations. His compositions are based upon Negro melodies, and I have encouraged him in this direction. The other members in the composition class seem to think that it is not in good taste to get ideas from the old plantation songs, but they are wrong, and I have tried to impress upon their minds the fact that the greatest composers have not considered it beneath their dignity to go to the humble folk songs for motifs.

"I did not come to America to interpret Beethoven or Wagner for the public. That is not my work and I would not waste any time on it. I came to discover what young Americans had in them and help them to express it. When the Negro minstrels are here again I intend to take my young composers with me and have them comment on the melodies."

CHAPTER VI

THE REASON WHY

By F. L. Barnett

The celebration of the four hundredth anniversary of the discovery of America is acknowledged to be our greatest National enterprise of the century. From the inception of the plan down to the magnificent demonstration of the opening day, every feature has had for its ultimate attainment the highest possible degree of success. The best minds were called upon to plan a work which should not only exceed all others in the magnitude of its scope, but which should at the same time surpass all former efforts in the excellence and completion of every detail.

No such enthusiasm ever inspired the American people to any work. From the humblest citizen to the Chief Magistrate of the Nation, the one all absorbing question seemed to be, "How shall America best present its greatness to the civilized world?" Selfishness abated its conflicting interests, rivalry merged itself into emulation and envy lost its tongue. An "era of good feeling" again dawned upon the land and with "Malice towards none and charity to all" the Nation moved to the work of preparing for the greatest Exposition the world has ever known.

The enthusiasm for the work which permeated every phase of our National life, especially inspired the colored people who saw in this great event their first opportunity to show what freedom and citizenship can do for a slave. Less than thirty years have elapsed since "Grim visaged war smoothed its wrinkled front," and left as a heritage of its short but eventful existence four millions of freedmen, now the Nation's wards. In its accounting to the world, none felt more keenly than the colored man, that America could not omit from the record the status of the former slave. He hoped that the American people with their never failing protestation of justice and fair play, would gladly respond to this call, and side by side with the magnificence of its industry, intelligence and wealth give evidence of its broad charity and splendid humane impulses. He recognized that during the twenty-five years past the United States in the field of politics and economics has had a work peculiar to itself. He knew that achievements of his country would interest the world, since no event of the century occurred in the life of any nation, of greater importance than the freedom and enfranchisement of the American slaves. He was anxious to respond to this interest by showing to the world, not only what America has done for the Negro, but what the Negro has done for himself.

It had been asserted that slavery was a divine institution, that the Negro, in the economy of nature, was predestinated to be a slave, and that he was so indolent and ignorant that his highest good could be attained only under the influence of a white master. The Negro wanted to show by his years of freedom, that his industry did not need the incentive of a master's whip, and that his intelligence was capable of successful self direction. It had been said that he was improvident and devoid of ambition, and that he would gradually lapse into barbarism. He wanted to show that in a quarter of a century, he had accumulated property to the value of two hundred million dollars, that his ambition had led him into every field of industry, and that capable men of his race had served his Nation well in the legislatures of a dozen states in both Houses of the Nation's Congress and as National Representatives abroad.

It had been said that the Negro was fit only for a "hewer of wood and a drawer of water" and that he could not be educated. In answer to this, the Negro wanted to show, that in a quarter of a century after emancipation, nearly one half of the race had learned to read and that in schools of higher education colored scholars had repeatedly won highest honors in contest with scholars of the dominant race. In a word, the Negro wanted to avail himself of the opportunity to prove to his friends that their years of unselfish work for him, as a slave, had been appreciated by him in his freedom, and that he was making every possible effort to gratify the sanguine expectations of his friends and incidentally to confound the wisdom of those who justified his oppression on the ground that God cursed Ham.

But herein he was doomed to be disappointed. In the very first steps of the Exposition work, the colored people were given to understand that they were *persona non grata*, so far as any participation in the directive energy of the Exposition was concerned. In order to Nationalize the Exposition the United States Congress by legislation in its behalf, provided for the appointment of a National Board of Commissioners, which Board should be constituted by the appointment of two Commissioners from each state, one from each territory and ten Commissioners at large. It was further provided that one alternate should be named for every commissioner. These appointments were made by the President of the United States (Benjamin Harrison) who thus had the appointment of a Board of National Commissioners numbering two hundred and eight members to represent the sixty millions of our population.

The colored people of our country number over seven and one half millions. In two of the states of the south the colored population exceeds the white population, and so far as the productive energy of the southern states is concerned, almost the entire output of agricultural products is the work of Negro labor. The colored people therefore thought that their numbers, more than one eighth of the entire population of the country, would entitle them to one Commissioner at Large, and that their importance as a labor factor in the South would secure for them fair representation among the Commissioners appointed from the states. But it was not so. President Harrison appointed his entire list of Commissioners, and their alternates, and refused to name one colored man. The President willfully ignored the millions of colored people in the country and thus established a precedent which remained inviolate through the entire term of Exposition work.

Finding themselves with no representation on the National Board, a number of applications were made to the direct management of the Exposition through the Director General, Hon. George R. Davis, for the appointment of some capable colored person, in some representative capacity to the end that the intelligent and enthusiastic co-operation of the colored people might be secured. The Director General declined to make any such appointment.

Prominent colored men suggested the establishment of a Department of Colored Exhibits in the Exposition. It was urged by them that nothing would so well evidence the progress of the colored people as an exhibit made entirely of the products of skill and industry of the race since emancipation. This suggestion was considered by the National Directors and it was decided that no separate exhibit for the colored people be permitted.

Recognizing that there was not much hope for successful work under authority of the Board of Directors, there was still a hope that in the work undertaken by the women there would be sympathy and a helpful influence for colored women. Unprecedented importance had been given to woman's work by the Congress of the United States, which in its World's Fair legislation provided for a Board of Lady Managers and set aside for their exclusive use sufficient money to make a most creditable exhibit of women's work. It was hoped that this Board would take especial interest in helping all aspiring womankind to show their best possible evidence of thrift and intelligent labor. It was therefore decided by colored women in various parts of the country to secure, if possible, means for making an exhibit that would partly compensate for the failure made in the attempt with the National Board of Directors. An idea of the plan of work suggested by these colored organizations can be had from one petition, addressed to the Lady Managers, from Chicago. It is as follows:

To the Board of Lady Managers,
World's Columbian Exposition,
Chicago, Illinois.

The Women's Columbian Auxiliary Association desires to bring its work properly before your honorable body, with a few suggestions which we hope may be of assistance in promoting the cause of woman's work among our colored citizens.

The above organization is working under a charter granted by the State of Illinois, and has perfected plans upon which it is working with the most gratifying success. Our membership in Chicago numbers nearly one hundred active, earnest workers, who have at heart the success of the women's department, and a creditable display of the skill and energy of the colored people.

Besides our city organization, the work has had the endorsement of two National Orders of a benevolent nature, and its work is being especially urged in that direction.

Much more will be done when we find that our plan of work meets the approval and has the endorsement of the Board of Lady Managers. To that end we desire to be accorded an audience with this body, or some representative of this body, who will give our work the consideration we believe it merits.

In the prosecution of our work, we have consulted some of the best minds of our race. We do not in any way suggest a separate department in the coming exposition, for colored people, but we do believe there is a field of labor among the colored people, in which members of the race can serve with special effectiveness and success.

Our ideas and plans in this connection are carefully outlined in a published prospectus for use of societies cooperating with us. We enclose a copy for your consideration.

Hoping to render you a service, in which we will gladly engage, We remain, respectfully,

Women's Columbian Auxiliary Association,
Mrs. R. D. Boone, Pres.

Prior to this movement, another society, by name the Woman's Columbian Association had filed a similar petition, through Mrs. Lettie Trent, its president. The two associations suggested work on nearly the same general plan, and contemplated work through various channels, such as secret societies, private schools and church organizations, which particularly reach the colored people. Naturally the two organizations had different leaders whom they endorsed and supported for the work, with more or less earnestness, fidelity and sometimes acerbity of temper, each of course, desiring its plans to succeed through the success of its representative. But both failed as the Board of Lady Managers eagerly availed itself of the opportunity to say that the colored people were divided into factions and it would be impolitic to recognize either faction.

The promptness which marked their assumption of this position, is fairly indicative of the hypocrisy and duplicity which the colored people met in every effort made. In refusing to give the colored people any representation whatever, upon the ground that they were not united, the Board made an excuse which was wholly unworthy of itself. The failure of the few colored people of Chicago to agree, could not by any kind of logic, justify the Board in ignoring the seven and one half millions outside of the city. A number of colored women in other sections of the country were highly endorsed and commended to the Board as capable, earnest and efficient representatives of the race. Because the few people here in Chicago did not agree upon the same person for their support the Board of Lady Managers ignored the plea of the entire race.

If in a reflective mood, the Lady Managers had read the minutes of their own organization, punctured as they are with points of order, cries of "shame," "shame," enlivened frequently with hysterics and bathed at times in tears, their sisterly love and sweetness of temper, marking a rose wreathed way through the law courts into Congress itself, possibly they would have been better able to realize that all people are liable to differ, and that colored people are not alone in their failure to agree upon the same person, to do a designated work.

But they never thought of such a possibility at that time. They dismissed the entire matter by referring the petitions of the colored people to the various State Boards.

With but a single exception the State Boards refused to take any action calculated to enlist the interest of the colored people. The State of New York, the exception referred to, appointed a capable and worthy colored woman, Miss Imogene Howard, as a member of the Board of Lady Managers. In the short period of her service she worked earnestly in behalf of her race, but met only with indifferent success.

The relegation of the interests of the colored people to the State Boards plainly proved that the Board of Lady Managers did not desire to have anything to do with the colored people. Still something was needed to be done and thousands of capable and conscientious colored men and women were waiting patiently for some suggestion of the work they might attempt to do. No suggestions came, however, and renewed efforts were exerted.

Miss Hallie Q. Brown, a teacher of Wilberforce College, Ohio, concluded to secure, if possible, from the several Lady Managers an expression of their views upon the subject of enlisting the interest and co-operation of the colored people in the formative work of the Fair. In pursuance of her plans, Miss Brown sent a letter of inquiry to each member of the Board of Lady Managers asking the personal consideration of her plan of appointing some colored person who would make this work a special care. The letter of Miss Brown reads as follows:

Chicago, Illinois, April 8, 1892.

Mrs. _____

Lady Manager of the Columbian Exposition for _____

Dear Madam:

It seems to be a settled conviction among the colored people, that no adequate opportunity is to be offered them for proper representation in the World's Fair. A circular recently issued and widely distributed makes that charge direct. That there is an element of truth in it seems apparent, since neither recognition has been granted, nor opportunity offered.

And further it is shown that the intercourse between the two races, particularly in the southern states, is so limited that the interchange of ideas is hardly seriously considered. If, therefore, the object of the Woman's Department of the Columbian Exposition is to present to the world the industrial and educational progress of the breadwinners—the wage women—how immeasurably incomplete will that work be without the exhibit of the thousands of the colored women of this country.

The question naturally arises, who is awakening an interest among our colored women, especially in the South where the masses are, and how many auxiliaries have been formed through which they may be advised of the movement that is intended to be so comprehensive and all inclusive? Considering the peculiar relation that the Negro sustains in this country, is it less than fair to request for him a special representation?

Presuming that such action would be had, several colored men and women, including the writer, have endorsements of unquestionable strength from all classes of American citizens. These endorsements are on file in the President's office of the Woman's Commission in this city.

It is urged at headquarters that the Lady Managers would seriously object to the appointment of a special representative to canvass the various states. Permit me to emphasize the fact, that this matter is in earnest discussion, among the representatives of eight millions of the population of the United States.

I address this circular to you, kindly requesting your opinion upon the suggestions made herein, and solicit a reply at your earliest convenience.

Yours respectfully,
4440 Langley Ave.   (Miss) Hallie Q. Brown
Chicago, Illinois.

The inquiry of Miss Brown received answers from less than one-half of the Lady Managers and in not more than three cases was any endorsement given to her suggestion to appoint some colored person to give especial attention to the work of securing exhibits from the colored people. In most of the answers received, the writers said that the appointment of a colored person could not be made without interfering with the work already assigned to the respective states. Several members excused the action of the Exposition Managers in refusing representation to the colored people among the promoters of the Exposition, by stating that the colored people themselves were divided upon the character of the exhibit which should be made; some declaring in favor of a separate colored exhibit, and others opposing it. Great emphasis was placed upon this statement and the further specious argument that colored people are citizens, and that it was against the policy of the Exposition to draw any distinction between different classes of American citizens. These arguments upon the first thought appear reasonable, but a slight consideration shows that they were made only as a subterfuge to compass the discrimination already planned.

The majority of the Lady Managers ignored the letters of inquiry entirely, while some were frank enough to speak their pronounced opposition to any plan which would bring them in contact with a colored representative and to emphasize the opposition by a declaration that they would resign in case such an appointment was made.

So far as the character of the exhibit was concerned there was an honest difference of opinion among both white and colored people, as to the manner of making the exhibit, some declaring in favor of a separate exhibit to be composed exclusively of products of the skill, ingenuity and industry of the colored people, others quite as earnestly opposed to any color line exhibit and insisted upon placing exhibits furnished by colored people in the classes to which they respectively belonged.

In support of the plan for the separate exhibit it was urged:

First: That the exhibits by the colored people would be so few in number, that when enstalled in their places as classified they would be almost unnoticed and as there would be no way of ascertaining that they were products of our skill and industry, the race would lose the credit of their production.

Second: That while the exhibits made by colored people would not compare favorably with the general exhibit of the white people, still in number, variety and excellence they would give most gratifying evidence of the capacity, industry and ambition of the race, showing what it had accomplished in the first third of a century of freedom.

The opponents to the separate exhibit, both colored and white, based their opposition upon the broad principle that merit knows no color line, and that colored people should be willing to be measured by the same rule which was applied to other people. The colored people asked that no special grade of merit be established for them; but held that the race was willing to accept whatever place was accorded it by virtue of the measure of merit shown. They asked that colored persons specially interested in the cause be appointed to promote the work among colored people, but that the exhibits when received, should be impartially judged and assigned to their places as classified.

But this was a question of method rather than action. The colored people were untiring in their demands for some responsible work, and were perfectly willing to allow the arrangement of details with the exposition management. But they earnestly maintained that whether the colored exhibits be installed in bulk or placed as properly classified, there was no doubt that the existing condition of public sentiment warranted the active assistance of colored representatives in promoting the work among colored people.

The fact patent to all thinking people that, in the first steps of exposition work they had been purposely ignored together with the equally apparent fact that the various State Boards, with one exception, had emphasized this slight by refusing to give any representation whatever to colored people, gave good ground for the belief that colored people were not wanted in any responsible connection with the Exposition work. But the demands for a separate exhibit and for the appointment of colored persons to assist in promoting the work of the exposition were all fruitless. They were met always with the statement that the exposition authorities had considered it best to act entirely without reference to any color line, that all citizens of all classes stood on the same plane, that no distinctions should be drawn between any classes and special work extended to none. This position which has every indication of justice would still be inequitable even if fairly maintained.

It may have been strictly just but it was certainly not equitable to compel the colored people who have been emancipated but thirty years to stand on the same plane with their masters who for two and one half centuries had enslaved them. Had the colored people of America enjoyed equal opportunities with the white people they would have asked in the Exposition no favor of any kind. But when it is remembered that only a few years ago the statutes of many of the states made it a misdemeanor to teach a colored person to read, it must be conceded that in no competition with the white man is it possible for the former slave to stand upon the same plane.

But the position taken was not only inequitable but was a false and shallow pretense. If no distinctions were to be drawn in favor of the colored man, then it was only fair that none should be drawn against him. Yet the whole history of the exposition is a record of discrimination against the colored people. President Harrison began it when with the appointment of more than two hundred and eight national commissioners and their alternates to represent the several states, he refused to appoint a single representative of seven and one half millions of colored people, more than one-eighth of the entire population of the United States.

When it was ascertained that the seals and glaciers of Alaska had been overlooked in the appointment of National Commissioners, it was a comparatively easy task for the President to manipulate matters so that he could give that far away land a representative on the National

Board. It was entirely different, however, with the colored people. When the fact was laid before the President that they had been ignored and were entirely unrepresented, he found his hands tied and the best he was ever willing to do thereafter to remedy the matter, was to appoint a colored man, Mr. Hale G. Parker, as an alternate commissioner from the State of Missouri.

In the appointments made on the Board of Lady Managers the discrimination was equally apparent, not a single colored woman being named on the Board proper and only one named on the entire list of members of the State Boards of management.

Taking these precedents for aid and comfort, the management of the Exposition found it easy to refuse to employ colored men or women in places of honor or emolument. Hundreds of clerks were necessary to carry on the work of preparation for the Exposition but all applications by colored men or women for clerical positions were politely received and tenderly pigeon-holed. Of the entire clerical force of the Exposition, only one colored man, Mr. J. E. Johnson ever received a clerical appointment. A clerical position was filled for a few months by Mrs. A. M. Curtis and soon after her resignation a similar place was filled by Mrs. Fannie B. Williams who was appointed only two months before the Exposition opened. These three clerical places constitute the best representation accorded the colored people during the entire Exposition period. This, in spite of the fact, that the propriety and justice of their employment was freely recognized and admitted. By vote of the Board of Reference and Control, the Director General was requested to report on the expediency of giving colored people a place in the great work. The minutes of the above Board show, that after a clear and forceful presentation of the claims of the colored people by Mrs. F. B. Williams the following resolution was adopted:

"*Resolved:* That the Director General be requested to lay before the Local Directory the expediency of having the department of Publicity and Promotion employ a colored man and a colored woman to promote the interests of the World's Columbian Exposition throughout the United States."

Whether the Board really meant anything by the resolution or not it is difficult to say, but certain it is that nothing was done. The expediency of the appointments was not questioned, but claim was made that there was not money to pay for the service. In fact a standing reply to suggestions for the employment of colored persons was the assertion that the Exposition had no fund which it could use for that purpose. It had no funds to meet the expenses contemplated in the suggestion made in the above quoted resolution of the Board of Control, yet it had actually and wantonly wasted nearly ninety thousand dollars in the construction of floats for use on opening day; which floats were discarded before they were finished and never used at all, their entire cost being an absolute and total loss of the entire sum of money used in their construction. The management readily found ninety thousand dollars to waste in this child's play, but could not find a fraction of that sum to meet a demand which was just, urgent and plainly apparent.

A final effort was made to secure the service of a good statistician whose duty it would be to prepare a statistical exhibit of the Negro since emancipation. The work mentioned could be done by colored people and would have contributed helpfully to the effort of proving our ability in all lines of thought and action. The appropriation asked for was only two thousand dollars, but the Board refused to allow that sum, and the plan was abandoned.

This unwritten law of discrimination was felt not only in higher places but its effects were seen in the employment of persons for positions of no more importance than the Columbian Guards. These were selected for duty on the Exposition grounds. The Commander, Col. Rice, requested a blank to be used in making applications, the questions asked being as carefully framed as those found upon the application blanks of an insurance company. It was noted that all colored applicants had some defect which disqualified them for service. This was more marked when so many colored persons were rejected who appeared to be eligible from every point of view, and from the further fact that many of the guards who were chosen clearly failed to meet the printed requirements, and a number of them could scarcely speak English. The rumor soon ripened into conviction, and it was generally understood that so far as the Columbian Guards were concerned, "No Negro need apply."

A sample of the treatment accorded colored applicants will serve to show that discrimination was undoubtedly practiced and was plainly intentional. The applicant in this case was Wm. J. Crawford of Chicago. He filled out his application blank and was soon ordered for examination. He reported and the examiner deliberately falsified the record and returned his report rejecting the applicant upon the ground that his chest measurement was only thirty-four inches, (the requirement being thirty-six inches) a report which he knew to be false. This action of the medical examiner was so clearly unjust that the applicant concluded to appeal to the Commander for a redress of the wrong. He prepared his appeal of which the following is a copy.

Chicago, Ill., March 5, 1893.

Col. Edward Rice,
Commander Columbian Guards,
World's Columbian Exposition.

Dear Sir:

I desire to ask your consideration of a matter, which I think, belongs to your department of the World's Fair. On the first day of the present month, I made an application for appointment on the force of guards for the exposition. My application was made on a blank furnished by Capt. Farnham, and I was ordered for examination.

The physician who examined me gave my height five feet eleven and one eighth inches; my weight one hundred and sixty-five and one half pounds, which was declared satisfactory. Upon examination for chest measurement, however, the examiner said that I measured thirty-four inches. He then said that this was too small and that I could not be accepted. He wrote on my application—"Rejected," adding "not on account of color, but because chest measurement not thirty-six inches."

I knew at the time that his mark was incorrect and as soon as I left the grounds, went to a reputable physician, who gave me a certificate of measurement of thirty-six and one half inches. As I was rejected because the examiner made my measurement thirty-four inches, I respectfully appeal to you for a reversal of that finding and an appointment upon the force of the Columbian Guards.

Obediently Yours,
W. J. Crawford.

This appeal was sent by registered letter to Commander Rice, and was receipted for by G. N. Farnham, his chief assistant. But the Commander gave no reply whatever to the appeal. Still determined to have a hearing, the applicant, after waiting ten days for an answer made an appeal to the President of the Board of Control. This second appeal was as follows:

Chicago, Ill., March 15, 1893.

To the President of the
Board of Control of the
World's Columbian Exposition,
Chicago, Illinois.

Dear Sir:

I have the honor to appeal to you for a consideration of my rejected application for a position as one of the Columbian Guards of the World's Columbian Exposition.

I have been a resident of Chicago for seven years and on the first day of March, 1893, I made a formal application and was subjected to the required examination by the medical examiner. At the conclusion of my examination, I was told by the examining surgeon that I had met every requirement and was in every way qualified except in the single point of chest measurement; the rule of the department requires a chest measurement of thirty-six inches, but the said medical examiner stated in his certificate of examination that my chest measurement was less than thirty-five inches, and further marked on said certificate the gratuitous information "not rejected on account of color."

I appeal to your honorable board for a reopening of my application for appointment as a Columbian Guard on the following grounds:

I am satisfied that my application was rejected solely on account of my color. I have been especially convinced that it is a case of mean and unjust discrimination against me, because, after leaving the World's Fair Grounds and the regular medical examiner in the employment of the Columbian Guard authority, I went to no less eminent physician than Dr. S. N. Davis of this city, and requested him to give me a careful and impartial examination as to my chest. I would respectfully refer you to Dr. Davis' certificate attached hereto. It will be seen that the finding of Dr. Davis' examination is in direct contradiction to the alleged measurement of the medical examiner at the World's Fair Grounds.

Although the said medical examiner at the World's Fair grounds laboriously stretched his tape measure and compressed my chest in every possible way, so as to force a short measurement, and in other ways aroused my suspicions as to his willingness to give me a fair examination, I did not feel justified in questioning his findings and appealing to you, until I had obtained an impartial examination from a physician, who could have no interest in me and my plans.

A further reason for this appeal to you is to call your attention to the fact that it is the settled policy on the part of the authorities in charge to make it impossible for any American Negro, however well qualified, to become a member of the force of Columbian Guards. It is a significant fact that every colored applicant, thus far, has been rejected for causes more or less trivial, or, as in my case, false.

I would respectfully state that before submitting this appeal to your Honorable Board, I duly applied to Colonel Rice, Commander in Chief of said Columbian Guards. Attached hereto please find a copy of the letter sent to Colonel Rice, but from which I received no reply. I also appealed to the Council of Administration and Control for a consideration of my claim, but I was refused a hearing.

It is believed by many of our people that this fixed policy of discrimination against us, is without the sanction and knowledge of the Board of Control, and as I have no means of redress from the injustice done me, as above set forth, I have determined to lay the matter before you, hoping that my appeal will be justly considered, and that I will be given a chance to win the position for which I have made due application, if I am qualified therefor.

Obediently yours,
No. 400 27th street.   W. J. Crawford.

It was merely an indication of the plan and policy of the Exposition Management that no notice whatever was taken of the respectful but, at the same time, convincing appeal made by Mr. Crawford. It had been determined that no colored man should be employed on the force of the Columbian Guards and that determination was not to be varied. The fact that one colored man had succeeded in discovering the contemptible duplicity and falsehood used to compass that purpose, made no difference in the plan, nor affected in any way its promoters. Theoretically open to all Americans, the Exposition practically is, literally and figuratively, a "White City," in the building of which the Colored American was allowed no helping hand, and in its glorious success he has no share.

Recognizing that the spirit and purpose of the local management of the Exposition were inimical to the interests of the colored people, leaders of the race made effective appeals to Congress and asked that the general government reserve out of its appropriation to the Exposition a sum of money to be used in making a Statistical Exhibit which should show the moral, educational and financial growth of the American Negro since his emancipation. The colored people recognized that the discrimination which prevented their active participation in the Exposition work could not be remedied, but they hoped that the Nation would take enough interest in its former slaves to spend a few thousand dollars in making an exhibit which would tell to the world what they as freedmen had done.

But here they were disappointed again. Congress refused to act. One appropriation bill passed the Senate and at another time an appropriation was made by the House of Representatives, but at no time did both bodies agree upon the same measure. The help that was expected from Congress failed and having failed in every other quarter to secure some worthy place in this great National undertaking the Colored American recognized the inevitable and accepted with the best grace possible one of the severest disappointments which has fallen to his lot.

In consideration of the color proof character of the Exposition Management it was the refinement of irony to set aside August 25th to be observed as "Colored People's Day." In this wonderful hive of National industry, representing an outlay of thirty million dollars, and numbering its employees by the thousands, only two colored persons could be found whose occupations were of a higher grade than that of janitor, laborer and porter, and these two only clerkships. Only as a menial is the Colored American to be seen—the Nation's deliberate and cowardly tribute to the Southern demand "to keep the Negro in his place." And yet in spite of this fact, the Colored Americans were expected to observe a designated day as their day—to rejoice and be exceeding glad. A few accepted the invitation, the majority did not.

Those who were present, by the faultless character of their service showed the splendid talent which prejudice had led the exposition to ignore; those who remained away evinced a spirit of manly independence which could but command respect. They saw no reason for rejoicing when they knew that America could find no representative place for a colored man, in all its work, and that it remained for the Republic of Hayti to give the only acceptable representation enjoyed by us in the Fair. That republic chose Frederick Douglass to represent it as Commissioner through which courtesy the Colored American received from a foreign power the place denied to him at home.

That we are not alone in the conviction that our country should have accorded an equal measure of recognition to one of its greatest citizens is evidenced by the following editorial in the Chicago *Herald* of Sunday, August 27th, 1893: "That a colored man, Douglass, Langston or Bruce, should have been named a National Commissioner, will be admitted by fair-minded Americans of all political parties. That President Harrison should have omitted to name one of them is apparently inexplicable. That the race has made extraordinary progress will also be conceded."

The World's Columbian Exposition draws to a close and that which has been done is without remedy. The colored people have no vindictiveness actuating them in this presentation of their side of this question, our only desire being to tell the reason why we have no part nor lot in the Exposition. Our failure to be represented is not of our own working and we can only hope that the spirit of freedom and fair play of which some Americans so loudly boast, will so inspire the Nation that in another great National endeavor the Colored American shall not plead for a place in vain.

TO THE PUBLIC.

This pamphlet is published by contribution from colored people of the United States. The haste necessary for the press, prevents the incorporation of interesting data showing the progress of the colored people in commercial lines.

Besides the cuts of a school and hospital it was desired to have a cut of the Capital Savings Bank, a flourishing institution conducted by the colored people of Washington, D. C. The cut, however, did not arrive in time for the press.

Twenty thousand copies of THE REASON WHY are now ready for gratuitous distribution. Applications by mail will enclose three cents for postage. All orders addressed to the undersigned will be promptly acknowledged. IDA B. WELLS,

Room 9, 128 Clark St.,

AUGUST 30, 1893. Chicago, Ill.

Back cover

Robert W. Rydell is a professor of history at Montana State University at Bozeman. He is the author of *All the World's a Fair* (1984) and *World of Fairs* (1993).

Typeset in 10.5/13 Adobe Caslon
with Memphis Extra Bold display
Designed by Dennis Roberts
Composed by Celia Shapland
for the University of Illinois Press
Manufactured by Cushing-Malloy, Inc.

DATE DUE

4/29/05			
4072106			

HIGHSMITH #45230

Printed
in USA